Why Bother?

HOW THE WORST PICKUP LINE OF MY LIFE
CHANGED MY FINANCIAL FUTURE AND
HOW IT WILL CHANGE YOURS TOO

BY PETER G. BIELAGUS

Printed in the United States of America

Bielagus, Peter

Why Bother? How The Worst Pickup Line of My Life Changed My Financial Future and How It Will Change Yours Too / by Peter G. Bielagus

Cover design by Blaine Lee

ISBN: 978-1-4675-1580-1

Warning – Disclaimer

ACKNOWLEDGEMENTS

I've stated before, in another book, that to say an author wrote a book is a bit of a lie. I'm referring to every author, not just the folks who use ghostwriters. I don't believe in ghostwriters. With so many Americans out of work, why would I employ the undead?

Anyway, though I wrote this book, many people contributed to its creation. Even larger is the list of people who contributed to my career, which contributed to me being able to write the book in the first place. Unfortunately, I will not get to all these folks here.

At the forefront of this battle, is my events coordinator, Rachel Jackson. She not only has to suffer through my horrendous spelling and grammar (even in an age of spelling and grammar checkers), run-on sentences, (and overuse of parentheses) she must suffer my hectic schedule as I conduct financial education seminars all over the world. For her tolerance, I thank her first.

My unpaid editors, Adam Ace and Andrew Roberts, my paid editors and designers, and Vervante, and my accommodating printers at Lightning Source. Also my business coaches, Larry Broughton and Phil Dyer and their associate Shawna Shoppe, who makes them look good. Special thanks to my literary agent (well manager to be technical) Ken Atchity, who "discovered" me many years ago and *still* hasn't given up on me. Also thanks to his staff at AEI, most notably Chi Li Wong and Brenna Lui.

Thank you as well to my family for their unwavering belief in a career choice that should've never worked out but somehow did. And finally, thank you dear reader for buying (or even borrowing) this book.

This book is dedicated to my nephew, Justin. If all of us (yes, you *and* me) manage our money smarter, the world will be a better place for him.

TABLE OF CONTENTS

Part 3: The Fun Stuff

Part 4: The Weird Stuff

Introduction

SO JUST WHAT WAS THE
WORST PICKUP LINE OF MY LIFE?

I know you want to read about the pickup line. But indulge me a page or two, because there is something I need to tell you first, and that is:

I have the greatest job in the world.

Okay, maybe that is a bit of an exaggeration, but only just a bit. I am not a rock star or a movie star, but I get as close as one can without having any music or acting talent. I'm a professional speaker.

I get to travel all over the world and talk to people about changing their financial lives. I have spoken in Greece, Italy, Spain, the Middle East, Japan, Korea, and even onboard an aircraft carrier at sea somewhere in the Indian Ocean. For the past seven years (going on eight), I have empowered students, service members, and professionals to change their financial lives.

One of the most rewarding parts of this shtick occurs long after I am done with the speech. Days, weeks, months, even *years* after I step off stage, people send emails telling me about how the speech changed their lives. Sometimes they'd tell me about a new financial triumph, like paying off a credit card. Other times they would email with a question. I always enjoyed these emails, because of their diversity, their honesty, and perhaps most of all, their positive nature. These emails were a coveted part of my business, and for years I'd greet each day anxious to fire up the old laptop and see who, if anyone, was checking in.

In 2008 that all changed. Mind you, my business didn't really change. I didn't really change. My revenues didn't really change. My clients didn't really change. It was the emails that changed.

They didn't change demographically. I still spoke to students, servicemembers and professionals. What started to change was their outlook. The emails started to contain statements like:

- *"There is no point in checking my credit score, because after the foreclosure I know it sucks."*
- *"I don't even open my brokerage statements anymore."*
- *"After the crash(es) of 2008, I stopped putting money into my 401k."*
- *"Here I am off to job interview number 20. Not sure what will be new about this one."*
- *"I don't even want to know how much I owe on my student loans."*
- *"Who's going to bail me out?"*

As 2008 grew into 2009, then 2010 and 2011, and still into 2012, emails like these started to become more and more frequent. Mind you, I still received many positive ones, mainly from young people for whom my talk was their first introduction to personal finance, but the bleak, hopeless, and forlorn camp swelled to an alarming number. Their emails accumulated into a rare reaction to the financial world, one that I had never seen before and one that could be summed up in two words: *Why bother?* Most difficult of all, at least for me personally, was that I was unsure of how to help these folks. After all, as I type this:

- More than 45 *million* Americans are on food stamps.[1]
- Federal debt is at an all-time high.
- There are a record number of foreclosed homes on the market.
- There are a record number of foreclosed homes *not yet* on the market (grimly referred to as the "shadow inventory").
- Students are graduating with record amounts of student loan debt.
- Unemployment floats around 10%.

[1] USDA Food and Nutrition Service website. www.fns.usda.gov

With news like this, it's tough to label these emailers as simply negative people. I did have tips I could send them, tips I felt would change their financial lives, but I realized I first needed to convince them it was worth trying.

That's when I remembered Charlotte.

I first met Charlotte my junior year of high school. She was a tall, tan, brunette whom I met for only one night. She was also the girl to whom I uttered the worst pickup line of my life.

The worst pick-up line of my life occurred when I was touring Southern Methodist University in Dallas, Texas. (All ready you know this is a true story. If I was lying, I would have said, "The worst pick-up line of my life occurred when I was touring Harvard, on a potential scholarship for football and biomechanical engineering.")

I can't remember why Southern Methodist University came up in my college search. I'm not Southern and I'm not Methodist, but I was looking for a university, so guess one out of three ain't bad. Anyway, there I was shuffling from building to building with my mom, along with 70 other kids and their parents.

After several hours of touring, we were corralled into a room where at one end boasted an impressive buffet. This was one of those uncomfortable "Hmmm, where do I sit" moments since no one knew anyone. You know these moments: You peer over your shoulder as you scoop buffet items onto your plate to see which table might be good fit for you. Fortune (for the moment) must have smiled on me because I spotted the perfect table. Perfect mainly because in one of the seats sat a striking young lady. A Southern belle burnished with a Texas tan, it was to this beauty that I would utter the worst pick-up line of my life.

"Hey Mom, let's go sit over there," I said, making the dash before someone else could grab the seats. Loyal to the bone, my mother cut out early from the buffet line and followed me, though I'm not sure if she knew what I was up to. You never know what moms are thinking; you just know they always know more than you think.

"May we join you?" I asked. Everyone had their mouths full, but they politely gestured to the open seats. As soon as we sat down and our tablemates had swallowed their food, introductions were made. I sat down and finally got a close look at this lovely lady, who for legal purposes, I've decided to call Charlotte[2].

I immediately attempted to make conversation, and I immediately ran into two problems. One was my mom, the other was her dad.

I know many people say this, but I do have the greatest mom in the world. She has always been there for my brother and me. My mother is the first person to offer her help and always the last person to give up on you. She seemed for the first 17 years of my life to be a woman without faults, but I finally saw a blemish on that fateful visit to Southern Methodist University.

She is not much of a wingman.

It is nice to have a wingman in situations like these. As you may already know, the job of a wingman is to play off and support the front man, (or point man depending on where you are from) to cover when he stumbles up, fill in if a silence arises, and if necessary, take one for the team. A solid point man/wing man team is unbeatable.

But a wing*mom*?

I knew it would only be a matter of time before she brought up the "Peter was such a fat baby" story (Oh yes, I was quite fat). My mom has little use for pick-up lines, but if she did, I'm sure this is what she would lead with. Such a story would violate the most primal rule of the wingman /point man relationship: *Never make fun of the point man.* I knew the clock was ticking until this story arose, so I had to get Charlotte alone.

As I said, my mom wasn't the only problem. Ashl- ... I mean Charlotte's dad was at the table. A hawkeyed patriarch, one whom I guessed wouldn't let any boy near his daughter, unless it was on bended knee. I assumed he had firearms in his home, most likely stored under his pillow, and perhaps he was even packing on the college visit. He was the type of guy who in high school probably scored four touchdowns in one game and NEVER LET YOU FORGET IT. He was dangerous mix of brashness and charm, and I knew with this titan at the table my chances were slim.

---

2   But if you're curious, her real name was Ashley.

But once again fortune smiled. After dinner, our college guide for the day deliberately separated students and parents into different Q&A groups. I arranged to sit next to Charlotte but found little time during this session to connect. I tried to think of a question, but the words wouldn't come out so long as she sat next to me.

After our Q&A, we were granted some "free time" to hang out in the warm Texas evening air. Ahhh ... this was my chance, my chance to talk with her, to connect, swap numbers or email. Maybe even ...

We dispersed out onto the quad in front of the building that still housed our parents. Circles inevitably began to form as the last thing anyone wanted to do was be caught standing alone. I lingered for a moment, for I knew this was it. Charlotte had yet to find a circle, and perhaps it was here and now that the fortune following me all night was going to complete this happy conspiracy.

It happened so fast. My brow began to sweat. My heart began to roar and all of a sudden, the sting of battle was once again upon me. I started my approach to her as she glanced around, wanting desperately to join a circle.

Five steps away. My blood grew hot.

Four steps away. She saw me coming.

Three steps away. I smiled

Two steps away. She smiled.

And upon that final step I uttered the worst pick-up line of my life.

"Hey Charlotte, listen do you want to –"

And then ... *nothing.* I said nothing. I literally stopped *mid-sentence* and stared at her. For upon that last step a monsoon of doubt overtook me. A monsoon summed up in two words, the same two words that have plagued my audience member emails since 2008:

Why bother?

I mean what was I going to do? We had five more minutes until they let us back into the room with our parents. WTF am I going to do in five minutes? "So what if we swap emails," I thought, "I don't even know if I am gonna go to this school. And look at her, she probably has a boyfriend." What's my line going to be, "Hey I know I met you for five minutes, and I know you live 800 miles away from me, but uhh can I have your number and uhhh maybe we could talk sometime?" This was well before Facebook, so I couldn't use that angle.

The negative thoughts consumed me to the point where I literally stopped my pick-up line mid-sentence. I never finished it. Charlotte asked me what I was going to say, and I just stared at her. Before I could answer, someone joined our circle of two, then another, and another. Then whatever shred of a chance I had at any intimacy with her was gone forever.

I want to be clear here. I did not lose my confidence mid sentence. That's happened before, but not this time. I did not stumble for words. That too has happened before, but not here.

You see dear reader, the worst pick-up line in my life was *not* something to the effect of "Is that a mirror in your pocket, because I can see myself ...," well you know the rest. It wasn't anything like, "That shirt is very becoming on you. Of course if I ..." and I'm sure you know the rest of that one, too.

No. The worst pick-up line of my life earned that title because I gave up. And I may just be the only man in the *country* who *consciously* decided to give up on his pick-up line *while in the middle of his pick-up line!* I didn't see how it could possibly work out with Charlotte and me. In the face of this conclusion, I did nothing.

In my travels all over the globe, speaking to students, servicemembers and professionals - from stay-at-home dads, to single working moms, doctors and entrepreneurs - people were asking me, "Why bother?

Many of you are feeling about your finances just as I felt when I was one step away from Charlotte. I know, I've received your emails. *Why bother?* is becoming a dangerously popular subject line. You may have lost your job, or walked right out of grad school with $100,000 in debt, straight into a job market that sentenced you to folding shirts at the mall (the same job you had *before* you got the graduate degree). Your business might have gone bankrupt, or the bank might have taken your home when the interest rate popped.[3]

As I mentioned, audience members have told me they don't even open their brokerage account statements anymore. They tell me their bank account is paying zero interest, they're headed to their 50th job interview with no inspiration left that this may actually be the one. College students delay calculating just how much they borrowed, and servicemembers are being attacked by predatory lenders more than ever before.

With 10% unemployment, 400,000-plus troops re-entering an already competitive workforce, massive federal debt, massive student loan debt, a gut-wrenching stock market, foreclosures that banks haven't even *started* processing yet, two political parties that *both* seem to be on the take as the haves and have-nots grow further and further apart, I mean let's get real here!

Why bother?

The reason you should bother, the point of this whole book actually, can be summed up in one sentence: There is always something you can do to improve your current financial situation regardless of what is happening in the outside world. It may not always work out the way you want it, but it certainly will work out better than doing nothing at all.

To this *day* I still wonder about Charlotte. What if I had asked for her number? Maybe she would have rejected me, a guy whom she knew for all of five minutes. If that was the case, then I wouldn't have worried about it ever again. But it still creeps into my brain, years later.

On the other hand, she could have said yes. She could have been my soul mate (assuming, of course, I believed in soul mates). The trouble is, because I chose to do nothing, I will never know.

---

3   Or perhaps you are confused about how to spend your government bailout-inspired Wall Street bonus, in which case you have the wrong book.

There is always something you can do to improve your current financial situation, regardless of what is happening in the outside world.

In the financial world, I do think we are in for a great shift. Whenever the economy touches too many extremes (extreme debt, extreme unemployment, extreme whatever) a great shift happens. The good news is that there are steps you can take to protect yourself and even profit from the shift, regardless of which way the shift goes. (More on how to get your shift together in Chapter 8.)

If however you do nothing, you might suffer a fate far worse than the chronic wondering I have over "woulda, shoulda, coulda" with Charlotte and me. You might get financially wiped out, and if you are already wiped out, you might lose the chance to recover rather quickly. Taking action is also inspiring, even when it fails. It gives you courage, hope, and belief – three things that are just as necessary to a healthy financial life as good credit, a cash reserve and the proper insurance.

I will not guarantee things will work out perfectly for you. They won't. But this book, if nothing else, will calm down some of the frustrations and hesitations you might have. It might even give you a few more peaceful nights. Should you actually follow the steps in this book, I think you will see more abundance in your life.

So I hope you will join me on this 200-or-so-page journey through the money maze. I hope even more, you will put some of the strategies into practice.

Oh and uhhh … Charlotte, if you are reading this, I would love another chance.

Part 1
The Simple Stuff

(ALSO KNOWN AS THE "YOU-HAVE-
NO-EXCUSE-*NOT*-TO-DO-THE-STUFF-IN-
THIS-SECTION-OF-THE-BOOK-BECAUSE-
IT'S-EASY-AND-QUICK-AND-COSTS-YOU-
NOTHING-SECTION.")

Chapter 1

THE ONE SLIGHT PROBLEM WITH READING PERSONAL FINANCE BOOKS

We now come to the point in the book where I am supposed to talk about the magic of compound interest. I am supposed to tell you the story of two twins, Saver Sally and her brother, Rascal Ralph, and their different investment plans. In case you haven't heard the tale, the old personal finance ditty goes that Saver Sally begins investing $500 a year on her 20th birthday. Rascal Ralph, on the other hand, waits to start investing until he turns 35 years old. To catch up, he begins investing $2,000 a year, or *four* times the amount Sally is investing.

Now I reveal the shocking conclusion. By putting in $2,000 a year for 30 years, Rascal Ralph invested a total of $66,000. When he turned 65 years old, Ralph has an impressive $396,000. But Saver Sally, who invested only $22,500, winds up with over $431,000. And then I am supposed to say something like:

"How did she do it folks? You guessed it! The magic of compound interest!"

I had a chapter and a story like this in my first book and in my second. Not to mention Suze, Dave, Eric, Jean, Andrew, Beth, Jane, and the other Dave[4] all have something to this affect in their personal finance books. I always thought this was a great story and many people were inspired by it.

Until 2008.

---

4   Suze Orman, David Bach, Eric Tyson, Jean Chatzky, Andrew Tobias, Beth Kobliner, Jane Bryant Quinn, and Dave Ramsey. Or if you prefer, Dave Ramsey can be "Dave" and David Bach can be "the other Dave." If you need more Daves, Dave Gardner from the Motley Fool, can be the other, *other* Dave.

After that, people became very skeptical about putting 10% of their money aside for 30 years to open the vault in the future and be greeted by a mountain of treasure. Personal finance books (including mine) can sometimes hug the formulas too tightly and not recognize the real world. So I will not tell you the story of Saver Sally and her careless brother Rascal Ralph. Instead, I will tell you the story of Old Gil.

Old Gil is a 20-year-old engineer who has only two pieces of luck in his life. The first is that right out of college he gets a job. The second is that he did read a personal finance book and decided, early on, to take control of his financial life. But other than that, just about everything goes wrong for Old Gil.[5]

Throughout his career, the only raise Old Gil gets is one that keeps pace with inflation. While it is a steady increase every year, he never gets a big bonus, never sees a double digit increase in his annual salary.

Old Gil's company has a retirement plan that matches 10% of what Old Gil puts into it. Old Gil read in that personal finance book that he should save 10% of his income, so he puts in $4,000 a year. His company matches 10% of that 10%, and so the account swells to $4,400. For 45 years, Old Gil's net return, after factoring in inflation, is *zero*. That's right, he pulls out only what he and his company put in. While his money kept pace with inflation, it did not grow at all. Not one cent.

When he turns 30, Old Gil buys a house for $200,000. Two years after he buys it, the price of it falls to $170,000. For 35 years, Old Gil lives in that house and like his retirement plan, the house *never* rises in value beyond what he paid for it. It simply keeps pace with inflation. After 35 years, it is worth $450,000 or $200,000 in today's dollars.

At age 35, Old Gil buys a rental property for $200,000. Again, the moment he buys it, it drops in price by $15,000. For 30 years, Gil rents out the property, but averages a *loss* of $100 a *month* for 30 *years*. That's right folks, Old Gil thought the property would be helping his cash flow, but the opposite is true: He loses $100 a month, every month, for 30 *years*.

If this weren't enough, two years before Old Gil is going to retire, Congress cuts his Social Security benefits in *half*. Poor Old Gil, right?

---

5   I am not sure why we are already calling him "Old" Gil, when at this point in the story he is only twenty years old. But let's go with it.

Well, maybe not.

Let's take a look at old Gil's situation. Currently he is 65 years old. His retirement account is worth $450,000.[6] While he had a zero percent return, he did keep pace with inflation so his $450,000 can buy what $198,000 could buy today. He also owns his home, free and clear for $450,000, or $200,000 in today's dollars (again inflation). The fair market rental of his home is about $3,000 a month, or $1,500 a month in today's dollars.

Old Gil also scored himself a rental property. Even though it lost him $36,000 over 30 years, he now owns it free and clear as well. It too never went up in value; it merely kept pace with inflation and is now worth about $450,000. Based on current rents, Gil could rent the property for $3,000 a month.

Assuming Old Gil is going to live another 20 years, here would be his situation:

- His retirement account is worth $450,000. Even if he continues to get *zero* growth, he would be able to spend $22,500 a year.
- He lives in his house and pays no rent, so one of his biggest expenses *is gone*.
- He rents his other house out and gets, after paying insurance, taxes and management fees, another $2,000 a month.
- Social Security, while cut severely, still yields him $1,000 a month.

So in total, Old Gil's income is $58,500. He earns about 70% of what he made while working as an engineer (adjusting for inflation.) But remember, as an engineer he had to pay for his house. Now he owns it free and clear, and it is no longer an expense. If, after 10 years of retirement, Old Gil needs more money, he can sell a house, or perhaps he works part time at a fun job. The point is, despite all that happened to him, *he did okay.*

---

6   Actually Gil did even better, but I am trying to be pessimistic in this story. I assumed he kept pace with inflation, and assumed inflation averaged just over 3% per year. But I did *not* count that Gil's salary went up every year, making his 10% contribution grow. I just kept the math simple, that every year he contributed $4,400. Also I didn't account for the tax breaks Old Gil got from investing in his retirement account, owning a home and owning an investment property.

It is possible, but unlikely, you will never get a raise. It is possible, but unlikely, that after 30 years your house will *never* do better than keep pace with inflation. It's also possible, but unlikely, that your rental property will lose you money 30 years in a row and never appreciate in value beyond inflation. It's also possible, and rather likely on this one, that Social Security will be cut in half or gone by the time you retire. It is possible, but unlikely, that after 45 years your investments - be they silver, gold, stocks, life insurance, or bonds - never go anywhere beyond the inflation rate.

And I admit it is possible, but *very* unlikely, that *all* of these things will happen to you as they did to the hero of our story, Old Gil. Even if they do, it is still worth plugging away because as we saw, Gil still did okay. Sure, he did not accumulate the coveted million dollars in his retirement account that he surely would have had if he had gotten a return of 8% for 45 years. He never hit it big in the real estate market. But most financial advisors believe you need to earn at least 70% of your income when you retire and have at least one home paid off. Old Gil hit that milestone, despite all the bad stuff that happened to him.

Mathematically, it is true that if you invest 10% of your income for 30 years and average a 7% return, then after 30 years, assuming you can keep earning that 7%, you will have accumulated enough money to replace your job. But we don't live in a mathematical world. We live in the real world. A world where 2008 happens. A world where we sometimes go from earning $70,000 a year to $30,000 a year and stay there for three years.

But despite the crazy ups and downs life throws at us, if you design a plan and stick to the plan, like Old Gil, you'll do fine. So let's get started!

You can always do something

I will be the first to admit a crash might be coming. But in a crash, not everything goes down. Some stuff goes up, and the harder the crash the higher that stuff will go. And if you are 45 years old and your retirement portfolio gets cut in half for eight years, were you planning on retiring in the next eight years? Even if you were, did you need 100% of that money in eight years? Probably not. Plan, don't panic. Spread your money out, focus on paying down your debt and keep reading.

Chapter 2

THE BIG IDEA

We learned from Old Gil that even when things don't work out perfectly, they still work out okay. Be consistent, stick with the big picture, and you'll get there. But what exactly is this big picture?

Personal finance is all about financing, or paying for your personal life. In order to pay for the things we love, like cable TV, smart phones, new shoes, ski trips, and *Twilight* memorabilia, we need money.

> Personal finance is all about financing, or paying for your personal life.

There are only two (legal) ways to get money:

1. Trade your time for money a.k.a. *working.*

2. Trade your money for money a.k.a. *investing.*

Most of us don't get to start out life with a whole bunch of money.

If you are one of those fortunate people where Option #1 needn't even be a consideration, you should probably put this book down and grab your favorite Rowling/Grisham/King/Meyer/Brown/Clancy/Ludlum bit and snuggle up with that.

The rest of us need to do some combination of both. For some, that could be getting money through 99.99% work and .01% investing, others might be able to start with a bit more of a cushion. It doesn't really matter where your numbers lie, most of us have to do some form of both.

There is a footnote to the goal of personal finance.[7] If it is all about financing, or paying for our personal lives, and if we need money to do that, we know that we can either invest for more money or work for more money. The footnote simply recognizes that you will not physically be able to work for the rest of your life. Your investments need to step in sometime before the day you die (and for far too many people it is the day of).

The process of personal finance couldn't be simpler because there are only four parts:

- **Income**
- **Expenses**
- **Assets**
- **Liabilities**

Income is any money that comes into your pocket. Your wages, dividends, interest, rental income, royalties, etc.

Expenses are any monies that leave your pocket. Things like cell phone bills, groceries and *Twilight* memorabilia.[8]

Assets are anything that, over the long term, will make you wealthier.

Liabilities are anything that, over the long term, will make you poorer.

The process then is to increase your income, while decreasing your expenses so you can purchase more assets, while avoiding or paying off your current liabilities, all so you can finance your personal life. In one

---

7   If it's a footnote, why am I not talking about it here?
8   I'm not letting this drop.

long sentence, that's it. But if it is that simple, why do so many people screw it up?

There are three reasons. The first is a misuse of the definitions of assets and liabilities. It's been said many times before, but no one took more flack for it than the "Rich Dad" author himself Robert Kiyosaki, when he claimed, "Your house is not an asset." People boiled over in rage when they heard that, scared that the single biggest investment of their lives was now something less. Kiyosaki uses a stricter definition of asset than I do, stating that an asset is anything that puts money into your pocket. Therefore a house, which *you* pay to live in, is not an asset. Had more people truly understood the definition (mine or his), a lot fewer overpriced houses would have been bought.[9]

The second reason is also inherent in the definition of personal finance. People say to me all the time, "If personal finance is about financing or paying for my personal life, well I have the money to do that now, so I'll just go do it." These people forget the footnote: that you won't be able to work forever, and even if you could, you may not want to.

And the final reason people screw this up is because, well, let's face it, *assets are boring.* Life insurance, bank CDs, stocks, even gold, are all boring compared to the liabilities they can buy like, fancy dinners, concert tickets, and flashy cars. So people skip the assets, or avoid them wherever possible, and go straight to the fun stuff. The ole, "dessert before dinner" strategy. It's no wonder so many people are in financial trouble.

My only counter to these reasons is to highlight the individuals, including myself, that did step up sooner rather than later to change their financial lives. I think as a whole we are a happier group, because we worry less about how to finance our personal lives. Taking chances (i.e. changing jobs, taking time off, starting a business) are all easier for us since we have a cushion of assets to rely on. Retirement doesn't seem that far off, and "semi retirement" is even closer. It's not too late for you. If you care to join us and become a little happier and less worried, keep reading.

We'll start with the most important question in personal finance.

---

9   I realize many people bought homes hoping to rent them out, or to sell them at a higher price later, both of which would qualify under our definitions. But what was missing was a true recognition that there are *no* permanently innate assets or liabilities. An asset can *become* a liability, and a liability can *become* an asset.

You can always do something

While many people blame catastrophic events like the stock market crash of 2008 or the mortgage crisis for their financial troubles, we as a nation *create* these troubles by ignoring the basics of personal finance: Increase income, decrease expenses, use this income to buy more assets, and pay down or get rid of liabilities. Easy.

Chapter 3

THE MOST IMPORTANT QUESTION IN PERSONAL FINANCE

The most important question in the world of personal finance is expressed in only two words:

Why bother?

Funny huh? This is the same question that became the impetus for this book. It's the question my audiences started to ask in an alarming number. But the strange thing is, it *is* the most important question in all of personal finance. Rather than frustrating you, it should *inspire* you.

Remember that personal finance is about financing, or paying for your personal life. But before you get too far into stocks, bonds, gold, real estate, life insurance, and you uncle's carrier pigeon pizza delivery business, you need to know *why* you should bother with them in the first place. What is the goal?

I know a lot of this sounds overly simple, but most people get the goal of personal finance backwards. They *personalize* their finances. People tend to get upset when the stock market goes down, even though their goal was not to touch those stocks for 30 years. Or they froth at the mouth because they are not "in" on a booming housing market, even though buying a house was not in their immediate plans.

Worst of all, they get angry at what they should have done. They wished they bought gold at $400 an ounce. They wished they sold their house in 2006. They wished they had bought stock in Apple when it was down. When they think about their finances, they get upset, which is the exact *opposite* result we are looking for when we manage our money.

The rest of this book is going to show you how to finance your personal life. But take a moment right now and define what that personal life looks like. Yep, I'm gonna ask you to write some goals down. Don't panic, goal writing has just five simple steps:

1. **Write your goals.** Well duh, but your goals should be specific and measurable. If you want a new car, describe the car in as much detail as you can. There is a big difference between a "car" and a Ferrari.

2. **Put a price tag on those goals.** Think about not only what it costs today, but what it will cost when you finally get around to buying it. Also think about what it will cost you to own it. Once you buy a boat, you're not done spending money, you've just begun![10] You have to clean it, insure it, store it, gas it up, and take your drunk friends out in it. Be sure to factor those costs in as well.

3. **Put a timeline as to when you want to achieve those goals.** Timelines increase motivation, so slap a date on all your dreams.

4. **Based on the above, prioritize those goals.** Trying to achieve all your goals at once is going to result in you achieving none of your goals at all. So decide which ones are important now and which can be done later (If you want my help in prioritizing, start with the goals that are truly assets – the stuff that will put more money in your pocket. Unsure of which are assets? Start by looking at the boring stuff.).

5. **Then write a plan to pay for those goals.** This doesn't need to be a volume of *War and Peace*. Keep it closer to *Tuesdays with Morrie*. It can be two or three simple lines. Just write enough so you'll know what the next step is.

To help you with your goals, on page 22 is Handy Dandy Form Number One. Feel free to plagiarize this, or any form in this book, at will. Put one goal per sheet. If you want to download a fresh copy, please visit the Resources section of my website www.peterbielagus.com.

---

10 Know what BOAT stands for? Break Out Another Thousand. ;-)

You can always do something

This will cost you nothing and it is the most important exercise in personal finance. If you don't know why you should care about your financial life, there's little point in reading anymore. Take 10 minutes and get started.

Handy Dandy Form #1: The Goal Sheet

Remember goals should be: Specific   Measurable

My goal is: _To open a Roth IRA account._

I would like to achieve this goal by: _the end of April (April 30th)_

The cost (if any) of this goal is likely to be: _$2,000_

In terms of my priorities, this goal is: (circle one)

(Urgent)   It Can Wait   Meh

People that may be able to help me achieve this goal are: _Dad_

My plan for achieving this goal is to: _Save my wages from Day One._

Chapter 4

LIST YOUR RESOURCES

Next time you are bored, type the words "One Red Paperclip" into your favorite search engine. If that search engine is worth its salt, you should be brought to the story of Kyle MacDonald.

Kyle MacDonald was a young man who wanted to own a home. He, like most people, ran smack into problemo numero uno[11] when it comes to buying a house. He didn't have the money. But Kyle has something just as good. He had one red paper clip.

His goal was to trade that paper clip for something, which happened to be a pen shaped like a fish. He then traded that fish shaped pen for something else, which happened to be a doorknob. A few trades later he had himself a Coleman stove. Still more trades and he had himself a ski mobile. You can read all about Kyle on his website www.oneredpaperclip.com or in his book of the same name. But let me tell you what I thought was his most interesting trade.

About three quarters of the way through his trading, he was the proud owner of a day with musician Alice Cooper. Kyle literally had a contract to spend the day with the rock legend. Surely this would be a valuable trade, especially to a diehard Alice Cooper fan. It could fetch a lot. So what did Kyle trade for it? That's right folks, you guessed it!

A snow globe.

A snow globe that, based on the picture I saw, could not have cost more than $100. When I was reading Kyle's story, I thought with this trade, he had blown the whole operation. That's when Corbin Bernsen intervened.

---

11   Translation: problem number one, for my nonbilingual readers.

Corbin Bernsen, for those of you not in the loop, is a long-established Hollywood actor, both on the big and little screens. From the 1980's hit *LA Law* to the *Major League* movies, to his current appearances on *Psych*, he's achieved the difficult task of being able to stay for decades in the world's most unforgiving town.

He also is a snow globe collector.

Bernsen traded Kyle a contract to appear in one of his movies for the snow globe. Kyle then traded the contract to appear in the movie to the town of Kipling, in Saskatchewan, Canada, for a house.

At the end of Kyle's story he asks you, "What is your one red paperclip?" In other words, what is that spark that will become a fire, or that seed that will become a tree? While that is a good question, I think Kyle's story teaches much more than that. Three things actually:

1. *You have more than you think.* Paperclips don't seem to be resources but Kyle proves they are. I confirmed this with my own eyes when I was on a safari in Tanzania, Africa. Halfway through the trek, I visited a Maasai village. As I stooped my head to get into the school house (read: hut) I noticed the tiny room had a blackboard at one end, which proudly displayed the English alphabet. I stared at the blackboard for a while because I couldn't help thinking something was unusual about it. After a few seconds, it hit me. No one ever wrote on it. It lacked the ever present eraser marks, those chalky clouds you see (or used to see before whiteboards) on blackboards in American schools. I was temporarily puzzled by this because blackboards, after all, are supposed to be written on, erased, and then written on again. But this blackboard had only been written on once. Again, the answer hit me like a thunderbolt: *They have no chalk.* I had to fly halfway around the world, take a five-hour Jeep ride deep into the Serengeti to realize I have more than I think. That chalk and paperclips and countless other items I carelessly toss around, are of immeasurable value to others. I hope you don't have to travel so far to realize this simple point. *You have more than you think.*

2. *What's worthless to you is of great value to others.* I thought Kyle had royally screwed up when he gave up the day with Alice Cooper for a snow globe. But that's because I hate snow globes.[12] Corbin Bernsen, thankfully, was a fan. And the town of Kipling had a house that was probably costing them money to insure and maintain, not to mention was not paying any property tax. It was a burden to them. But to Kyle, it was a dream. If you can truly accept this, then the arguments of "there is only so much to go around" goes out the window. Synergy can happen because we don't all want the same things. If we stop and took a moment to decide what was truly important, and a second moment to decide what we should get rid of, then the world becomes an abundant place.

3. *Resources are the same as money.* As a financial speaker who specializes in people with modest incomes (young professionals, students, and service members), I constantly hear people tell me they are broke. When they say this to me, however, they are only counting the dollars they have (or don't have) in their pockets. They are not counting their resources, things like, talents, skills, education, ideas, and red paperclips. When financial planners ask you to determine your net worth, they don't allow you to count your resources, and I feel they should. So let's do it.

Take a moment and list out all of your assets and liabilities. Feel free to use the Net Worth Worksheets to help you get started. This is the exercise all financial advisors will make you do, and I admit it is a good one. But I want you to keep going, using the following sheet to list *all* of your resources. These could be non-tangible items, like ideas, friendships and skills, or they could be physical items, like a lawnmower or an antique rug. In the next chapter, we're going to figure out what to do with those resources.

---

12   Okay, "hate" is a strong word. I should say I have no affection for them.

Handy Dandy Form #2: Your Net Worth

Assets:

Current value of retirement brokerage accounts: _____

Current value of non retirement brokerage accounts: _____

Current value of home: _____

Current value of all precious metals: _____

Cash value of life insurance policy: _____

Current value of rental property(s): _____

Current balance in checking account(s): _____

Current balance in savings account(s): _____

Current value of bonds not in brokerage account: _____

Value of business: _____

Other assets: _____

Total Assets: _____

Liabilities:

Home Loan(s): _____

Student loans: _____

Credit card balances: _____

Car loan: _____

Rental property loan: _____

Business loan: _____

Payday loan: (I hope not!) _____

Other loans: _____

Total Liabilities: _____

Grand Total (Assets minus Liabilities): _____

Don't panic! Regardless of what that number looks like, remember, we're not done. Time to start listing your resources. Oh BTW, what's my definition of a resource? Here ya go: *Anything that can help you or others lower liabilities and increase assets.* A resource then is still a resource, even if it is not valuable to *you*. I'll get you started, and then you run with it:

Handy Dandy Form #3: Your Resources

People I know (movers, shakers, Popsicle makers):_____

_____

_____

_____

_____

_____

The last three brilliant ideas I had (but never did anything with):

_____

_____

_____

_____

_____

_____

Three things I am wicked good at:[13]_____

_____

_____

_____

_____

_____

---

13   For all you non- New Englanders out there, the term "wicked" is used to emphasize an extreme.

Three physical objects I own that are of immeasurable value to me:

_____

_____

_____

_____

_____

_____

Three physical objects I own that I don't really need but someone else would love: _____

_____

_____

_____

_____

_____

Okay, I got you started. The rest is up to you. Keep going and see just how much you really have.

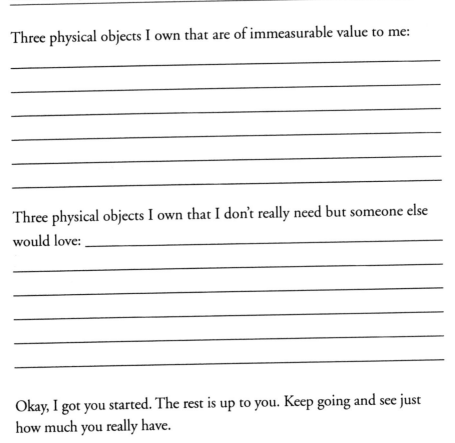

You can always do something

I realize people hear the story of Kyle MacDonald and think, "Yeah, he just had one of those million dollar ideas and coasted off the publicity. You can't do that every day. Not *everything* is a resource." I agree. Although Gary Dahl, the creator of the Pet Rock made a fortune selling, err…rocks. But yes that's one … well, Paul Hartunian also made a fortune by selling the scrap wood from the Brooklyn Bridge. Yep, he was the first man in history to *literally* sell the Brooklyn Bridge. But that's just three people: Kyle, Gary and Paul. Oh well, there's also Alex Tew, who designed the "million dollar website" by selling ads of 1 pixel per ad at a cost of $1. (Google him.) But these people just got lucky. Right?

Chapter 5

LIGHTEN UP

Most of us have too much crap in our lives. This alone should be a crime, but it gets worse. Many of us are paying to store our crap, either in a larger home or apartment than we really need, or in one of those self storage facilities. These two things – the fact that we have too much crap and that we pay to store it – is a truly heinous crime, but it gets even worse.[14] Much of this crap that we have, *we hardly care about.* And yet it still gets worse, because as the last chapter revealed, what is borderline worthless to us may be a treasure trove for someone else.

So lighten up!

Go through your home, apartment, dorm room, trailer, tree house, even your car and start getting rid of your crap. If you can sell it, great! If you can trade it for something more valuable, that's great too. If you can donate it, wonderful. If you can recycle it, that'll work. And if you have to flat out chuck it, then do it. Having "stuff" for the sole sake of having it interferes with your financial plans.

Don't believe me? Just look at your goals. Do any of you goals read: "Keep all the clothes that are in my closet?" "Keep paying for my self storage shed until the year 2045?" Probably not. In fact I'll wager your goals read just the opposite like, "cut expenses" or "have more free time." We have to pay to insure our stuff, store our stuff, and clean our stuff. We waste time caring for our stuff and cleaning *around* our stuff (ever try dusting around shelf full of knickknacks? It takes forever).

---

14   Always wanted to use the word "heinous" in a book. Now I finally did!

TRUE STORY

Several years ago I spent three weeks backpacking through Vietnam. I did not have any checked baggage; everything fit in my carry on for three weeks. When I got home, my parents asked me if I had any regrets about the trip. I had only one: I brought too much crap.

You can always do something

Remember that dress you wore only once to your friend's wedding? Are you going to wear it again? If not, someone out there would consider receipt of that a fairy tale come true. That pasta maker you bought off the Home Shopping Network? Come on, did you ever actually make any pasta? I know you tried it once, but you screwed it up remember? Give that pasta maker to someone who will make good use of it. Maybe that's your neighbor, maybe that's a soup kitchen. Whoever it is, lighten up.

Chapter 6

BUDGETING/SPENDING/SAVING

Every one of the 300 books I read on personal finance spoke about creating a budget. The problem is when you ask the average person about their cash flow, they typically have no idea where it all goes. Budgets are terrific when they work, but they so often don't, so the question is:

Why?

I found there are three reasons. The first reason is that we typically write our budgets in La La Land. Often we write down what we *want* to spend on groceries, rather than what we actually spend. We assume our cars will never break down, that we'll never get stuck at the airport and have to pay for a hotel out of our own pockets, or that we'll never screw up in our relationships thereby creating a costly order of "I'm sorry" flowers. These things happen. I know, I am on a first-name basis with my florist.

For most people, a budget is a list of expenses you *all ready* know.

The second reason is that budgets don't contain the little stuff. People don't forget they have to pay rent. It doesn't slip their mind that they have a car loan. No one thinks they are earning the wages of a plastic surgeon, when in fact they are a social worker.

No, what kills us are the little things. That bag of chips out of the machine at 3 o'clock. The morning coffee. That DVD you rented (even though you have Netflix).

Number three is a law I coined "Chain Reaction Shopping." This law states that one purchase just leads us to more purchases. Buy a new TV, and you get the warranty.[15] Purchase a new car and you just signed up for higher registration fees, higher insurance premiums, loan payments and taxes. Or my favorite, the cell phone. We are constantly bombarded with ads of how to get "1000 anytime minutes for $29.95 per month." But according to JD Power and Associates, the average American cell phone bill is $77 a month. What happened? Taxes, texting, global email, monthly insurance, and Angry Birds is what happened.

If you wrote a budget, however, you probably put $29.95 per month, because that's what your plan is. Chain reaction screws up our budgets because we fail to think about the purchase *behind* the purchase.

So what do you do?

But enough about why budgets don't work. The real question is: How do I fight back? I suggest most people start by writing three lists. The first two are easy, the last one is tough. Here they are:

- **List #1: A list of what's important to you:** This is slightly different than the goal sheet you (hopefully) wrote in Chapter 3 because this list does include little things, like shaving cream or pasta sauce. If those two things are important to you, put them on this list, right alongside your big goals like Ferrari and summer home.

- **List #2: A list of what's NOT important to you:** While every finance book tells you to write down what you want to spend your money on, I am the only guy in town who asks people to write down what they *don't* care about. Do you care *which* gas

---

15   But don't get the warranty. Statistically speaking, it's not worth it.

station you buy your gas from? Do you care which brand of fabric softener you use? If not, put it on this list. What's important about this list is that it will help you avoid the impulse purchase. The high-priced, brand name fabric softener (heck the high-priced anything) is right in front of you, at eye level, easily reachable and in a bright colored box. The cheap stuff is way down by your knees or over your head. But the pricey stuff is easy to get, which is why so many of us reach for it (often singing the accompanying jingle in our heads). Marketers spend *billions* to make sure you do just that. They way to fight back is with a written list, which will eventually melt into a mental list of everything you could care less about. When you are about to grab that overpriced brand name item, the list will kick in and remind you to buy the cheap stuff.[16]

- **List #3 (The Tough One) A list of where your money is going every single day:** Take an average month of your life (and I know you won't do a whole month, so at least do a week) and write down *everything* you spend money on. You put 35 cents into a parking meter, write it down. Buy a soda out of the machine? Write that down, too. Took a cab instead of the train? Write that down or get a receipt. When your week or month is over, total all your items into a list.

The real wow comes when you compare these three lists side by side. You will notice that what you want is actually not what you spend your money on every day. Most people don't have "Bag O Chips" on their "Important List." Yet every day at 3 o' clock, you and Old Gil take a stroll down to the cafeteria and buy a snack.[17]

Even worse, sometimes the items on List #3 actually appear on List #2.[18] We are spending money on stuff we consciously don't want; yet so powerful is the juggernaut of marketers that we easily part with our money.

But this isn't about shock value. This is about putting more money in your pocket. Simply by writing these three lists, you will be ahead of the game, since it will affect your subconscious the next time a marketer tries

---

16   Come on, you can do this. Think. Toothpaste? Toilet paper? Can you honestly tell a good vodka? Especially if it's your third one?
17   Wait, you *work* with Old Gil?
18   There's a reason it's called List #2

to dazzle you. It also will be a wake-up call, clueing you in on just how much you spend on things you had no idea you spent this kind of money on.[19] It will help you fill in the gaps of your budget, the "little stuff" we so often miss.

The lists can do even more if you want to work them. Take list #1. This is everything in your life that you want. Take each item on that list and figure out if there is a cheaper way to get it. If you want some help jumpstarting your brain, here are seven questions to ask of every item on List #1:

1. Can I buy less of it?

2. Can I buy a different brand but still get the same product? (Remember many companies that make brand name products also make a store brand, which, chemically, is the _exact_ same product.)

3. Can I buy it out of season? (Buy snow skis in July and swimsuits in December?)

4. Can I buy it on subscription? (While most common with newspapers and magazines, this could be applied to anything.)

5. Can I buy it in bulk? (Everyone knows to buy toilet paper in bulk, but what about getting a few friends together and buying _cars_ in bulk?)

6. Can I buy it from a different source? (Often you can get the same product cheaper by going online, buying it from a used dealer, or at a discount store.)

7. Can I not buy it? (Look at the item again. Is it truly important to you?)

List #2 provides a tally of hints on where to cut back. If, for instance, you don't care about where your coffee comes from, as long as you get your caffeine fix, then you'll know to brew at home.

For the extremist: Micro-budgeting

Micro-budgeting is a simple but rather extreme form of budgeting. It's a last resort for those who simply cannot make anything else work. While most budgets ask people to think in terms of months or weeks, a

---

19 When I first did this, I discovered I spent $350 in one month on taxi cabs.

micro-budget is a budget for a *day*.

The most radical version of micro-budgeting has five steps:

1. Pick an amount of money you will spend each day for a week. Say $20 a day.

2. Get this amount of money in cash from the bank. (For the whole week.)

3. Every morning, take your ID, your cell phone and the daily amount with you, and leave all credit cards and debit cards at home.

4. If you blow all your money by 2 p.m., you cannot spend anymore for the day. You'll have to eat what is in the fridge for dinner.

5. If, however, you have $3 left over by midnight, you can allocate that $3 for the next day (or you can put it into a savings account for a big purchase).

Extreme, but simple. You cannot get into trouble with this simply because you are not carrying the means to overspend. Those items that contribute to overspending - credit cards, debit cards and check books - were left at home. If you run into the much ballyhooed "emergency," you always have your cell phone to save you.

For more great savings strategies, please visit the Resources section of my website www.peterbielagus.com.

Of course, we didn't talk about all the "traditional" budgeting strategies here, like writing down your fixed monthly and yearly expenses. You need to do that, even if it hasn't worked before. Hopefully the new techniques outlined in this Chapter will change that.

You can always do something

If you've tried budgets and they haven't worked for you, then it's time to try something else. This chapter doesn't ask you to cut back on anything that you truly want. It's only asking you to figure out what's truly important. Know that and you'll soon have more money.

Chapter 7

HOW TO PUT SOME MONEY IN YOUR POCKET QUICKLY AND EASILY

There is no free money out there. Sorry, I've looked. But thankfully, there is money you've already spent that you can get back. This chapter will help you find it. To do that, we'll have to start with a quick discussion about Kim Kardashian.

Suppose, when she moved to New York, Kim Kardashian paid a $50 deposit to have her cable hooked up. Once the cable company receives the deposit, they send over a dude, who is scheduled to arrive sometime between 8 a.m. and noon. He arrives at 11:59 a.m. and hooks up the cable. From there, Kim pays her bill on time month after month.

Suddenly, she gets an urgent request to head back to L.A. She cancels her cable, breaks her apartment lease and bolts for the City of Angels. In the blink of an eye, she's gone.

But ...

The cable company is still holding her $50 deposit. Legally, they are not allowed to keep it because Kim always paid on time. At this point the cable company has two choices. They can try to track down Kim's address in L.A. and send her the money. Legally, they must at least attempt this option. If they fail, there is a backup - they can give it to the unclaimed funds office of the New York State Treasury Department.

Every state has a treasury department, and every department has an unclaimed funds office. This is where all this missing money - forgotten deposits, uncashed checks, abandoned property, unclaimed assets in safety deposit boxes - winds up. Once it lands in the unclaimed funds office, it becomes the state's problem to track you down.

Thankfully, several years ago, a guy by the name of Al Gore invented something called the Internet, and now every state in the nation has put its unclaimed funds/ abandoned property database online. You can easily search every state you have ever lived in all from one website.

Drum roll please. That website is www.unclaimed.org. Now this is the *only* website I want you to go to. There are other websites - and I am sure you have received ample amounts of their spam email. Please avoid them. Many of these websites charge a fee to find stuff you can easily find for free.

But does it *really* work? If I may indulge you with a few true tales from the front lines:

From Dushawn, a student who attended my speech at the University of Michigan, Flint:

I just wanted to say thank you for the advice. I searched for my dad and he had a check owed to him from the military for $6,500.00. He is claiming it now.

From Joseph at Georgia Southern University: (I like this one, very DaVinci Code-ish)

I checked out the <u>unclaimed.org</u> and my deceased father had some secret safety deposit boxes that no one knew about. I am planning a trip to Tennessee to check it all out.

From Tim, a reader of my blog, commenting on what his brother found:

BTW Jon found $3,200 on unclaimed property …

BTW, how did *I* do? Well not as good as these folks, but I did get $17.77 from my cable company. And who knows how well you will do? But who cares? It's *your* money. Currently there are over $32 *billion* dollars in unclaimed funds sitting in all the state treasury accounts. Take a moment to get your share.[20]

---

20   Oh I should mention that you can type in other people's names on this website. Mom's, dad's, Uncle Ted's, even Kim Kardashian's name. As I write this, Kim is owed $54.19 by the Malibu branch of Bank of America.

Still more money...

All right, let's get you some more money. We need to talk about the great shift in retail. Though I am not sure when the great shift in retail happened, I know that at some point, retailers began offering discounts in exchange for loyalty. Discounts always existed to move unwanted merchandise, but that wasn't enough for retailers. They wanted your soul.

Well, at least your wallet. So loyalty clubs started springing up. You know these, rent ten movies your eleventh one is free, frequent flier miles, hotel points, all that jazz. If you use the companies enough these extra perks really add up. The trouble is very few of us spend that much money at any one company to really make the points mean much. What we *really* need is one loyalty program that includes hundreds of companies.

And now we have one. Well, three actually (and there are even more). For the moment, I will talk about my favorite. It's called www.upromise.com, and it was *originally* created to help people with the astronomical increase in college tuition. I, however, prefer to use its little known, built-in loophole.[21]

Here's how it works. Upromise went around and made deals with a ton of big brand name corporations like Staples, Exxon Mobile, CVS, and Coca-Cola. Ever heard of them? These corporations agreed to give rebates back to Upromise members whenever members buy these products. But they don't give you the rebate at the cash register. Instead, these rebates get swept into your Upromise account. Once the money is in your Upromise account, it's yours, fo' free.

You can join Upromise by logging onto their site and opening up an account. (That's free, too.) They suggest that you register your debit cards, your credit cards, and your store rewards cards (like your drug store card or your grocery store card). Basically the website keeps track of these card numbers. When one of these numbers is used to buy a product from one of Upromise's participating vendors, a small percentage of your purchase goes into your Upromise account.

Here's an example. Let's say you go to Upromise and register your VISA credit card. The website is now watching whenever you use that card. Let's say you fill up your gas tank at Exxon Mobile for $20 and you

---

21   Mwhahahahahahahahaha!!!!

pay with your Visa. What happens is 1% or 20 cents, of what you spend at Exxon gets swept into your Upromise account. That's your free rebate. If later that day you used your VISA to buy something at Bed Bath and Beyond, then 2% would get swept into your Upromise account. As you spend with the registered cards at Upromise's vendor affiliates, small amounts of money keep getting swept into your account. It is totally free and it is totally yours.

When you log onto the website www.upromise.com, you're going to see the words "colleges savings" or "save for college" plastered everywhere. There will be pictures of babies as well. Remember, the site was originally designed to help people save money for college so they target mothers. The company hopes its members will take the money they accumulate from their rebates and put it into what is known as a 529 college savings plan. The loophole is that you can simply send a letter at any time to Upromise.com requesting that they send you the money in your account. And they will.

What's the catch? Well there are three as I see it:

1. It does take an offensibly long time to get your check. Somewhere around 12 weeks.

2. You will get a dash more email. But what's another two emails a day on top of the 750 you already get? Plus, it's not spam, it is highlighting additional discounts at the places you shop.

3. They are watching. Yes, now companies will know even *more* about you. But they are trying to track this stuff anyway. Might as well get paid for it!

If you are cool with the above, Upromise can help you get back some nickels, dimes and even quarters on nearly everything you buy. I've found, as a lifetime average, people can earn about $100 a year. Some will earn more, some less, but it requires no effort and the money is all nontaxable![22]

Two other sites that work just like Upromise are babymint.com and igive.com. Babymint (again targeting new mothers with college savings on their mind) has fewer companies than Upromise, but often has higher

---

22   Why? Because only *income* is taxable. This money is not income, it is a rebate.

contribution percentages (some as high as 10% of the purchase price!) Igive is a bit different in that the money does not go to you; it goes to the charity of your choice. This site has *already* given away over $2 million just by shaving pennies off of people's purchases.

You can always do something

STOP reading and go to unclaimed.org. Put in your name, your spouse's name, your girlfriend's name, and your girlfriend's ex boyfriend's former pet owner's college roommate's name. See what you and those you love are entitled to. Then take a few minutes and register at Upromise and the other sites. Who knows what free money lies out there for you?

Chapter 8

HOW TO GET YOUR SHIFT TOGETHER

Imagine you had $100,000 to invest.[23] Unsure of exactly where to put your money you decide to take $500 of it and invest it in an investment conference coming to town. You book a hotel room near the convention center, check in, and sleep soundly knowing that tomorrow you will have all the information you need to maximize your $100,000.

The first seminar of the day is all about investing in gold and silver. The presenter makes a very convincing argument as to why the U.S. dollar is going to collapse. The government is literally printing money, and pretty soon nations are going to catch on to this sleight of hand and stop accepting U.S. dollars. "They'll call our bluff," the presenter will say, "just as Charles De Gaulle did in the late 1960's when he demanded the gold that the U.S. dollar was supposedly backed by."[24] Chart after chart is piled upon you until you leave the session completely convinced that gold and silver are the best places for your money.

Session number two, however, is all about deflation. This happens when the value of stuff starts to go down. The presenter of this workshop speaks a lot about Japan and how they suffered through a tremendous period of deflation, mainly because their prices were so high to begin with. She has a lot of faith in the U.S. dollar and argues that the Euro is in far worse shape. Gold, she says, is at an all-time high, and the dollar is the safe haven everyone will turn to when metals come crashing down. She suggests you buy long term Treasury Bonds, which do well in periods

---

23   I know I know. Just go with me here.
24   In this case the presenter would be right. De Gaulle's demand actually forced Richard Nixon to completely abandon the gold standard. Nixon claimed this was a temporary measure, temporary in this case meaning several decades. More on the gold standard later.

of deflation. The only problem is *that is the exact opposite* of what the gold guy told you!

You leave session two scratching your head as you grab a seat at the back of the room for session three. This workshop is all about opportunities in real estate. The presenter could not be more excited. "Ya know what these record foreclosures in real estate mean for you folks?" he shouts. "Buying opportunities!" He explains how prices are in the toilet and interest rates are at an all time low. You learn how you can buy properties with no money down. Forget gold, forget the U.S. dollar. The money is in real estate.

That's the thought, anyway, until you go to session four. Again Japan comes up and you are reminded of how their real estate market declined for 19 *years*. The presenter also recaps that there are *millions* of properties that should be in foreclosure, the banks just haven't gotten around to them yet. She calls them "shadow foreclosures" and adds, "You can't believe the foreclosure numbers, folks. It's even worse."

Frustrated, you sneak out of this presentation to listen to another guy talk about stocks. When in doubt, buy stocks. But the news is just as bad. The presenter, through a collage of charts and graphs, argues about how the Dow Jones Industrial Average - the index that supposedly speaks for the whole stock market - should be at 3,000 when it is currently at 12,000. Because the Baby Boomers are starting to retire, he explains, they will pull their money out of the stock market in the greatest exodus since Moses. Massive selling means the market is going to plunge, leaving investors with one quarter of their money.

By the end of the convention you are even more confused about what to do. Should you sell your house? Buy gold? Buy stocks? Sell your stocks? Hold cash? Get rid of your cash? Become a monk? Get thee to a nunnery?[25]

There is good news. News that the presenters didn't tell you because they A) were probably salespeople trying to get you to buy their one thing and not the other guy's thing and B) don't work together and look at your financial life as a whole. They didn't tell you about the "Floor and Ceiling" principle.

---

25 With these numbers, the monk/nun option is looking pretty good.

Suppose you leave the convention utterly confused and you decide not to decide at all. Instead of choosing between all the investments you heard about in the presentations of gold, stocks, real estate, bonds, cash, and cash value life insurance (all of which you'll read about in this book), you simply decide to buy them *all*. You take your $100,000 and divide evenly so that about $15,000 goes into every investment. You also make a commitment to make one extra payment a year on all of your debts (your house, your car, etc).

Let's just pretend the gold guy is right. Gold goes up five times its current price. Your stocks lose half their value, the value of your house stays the same because of inflation, but the market is still terrible. You real estate stocks do fairly well for this reason, doubling in value. Your life insurance takes a hit in the bond market, but the policy is guaranteed, so the value stays pretty much where it is. With inflation, the value of your dollar goes down, so your cash will only buy you 70% of what it could before, and when interest rates go up (as they often do in times in high inflation) bond prices go down, so you get clobbered in the bond market, losing *half* your value.

But here's the kicker, you are still *up* $54,000! Your investments can only drop to zero (the floor), but there is no limit as to how high they can go (the ceiling).[26] We could just as easily play this game of "if the stock guy was right" or "if the real estate guy was right," the same way I look back at that fateful day of my tour at Southern Methodist University. Don't forget, in our example you committed to paying off your debt faster than usual, and that's not even counted here.

Is it this simple? Of course not. But it is also not as complex as people make it out to be. You have essentially two options:

1. **Always try to find The Next Big Thing.** When stocks are hot, you're in stocks. You get out of stocks before they crash, because you are already onto The Next Big Thing. The Next Big Thing

---

26 And it is very rare for an investment to go to zero.* Investors who rode the elevator to Hell in great collapse of Bear Stearns still walked away with $10 a share. That hurts considering it was at $132 that same year but it's still not zero.
*As a footnote to this footnote (can you even do that?) I do realize that many people have homes that are underwater, meaning it can go less than zero. Other investments, short the stock market and writing naked calls, also provide opportunities for you to lose more than you put in. While I cannot undo what has already been done, there are steps to take to protect yourself from these downswings – steps we'll discuss in this book.

starts to wear out its welcome and you then are onto The *Next* Next Big Thing. Round and round you go, hopping from one investment to the other, always at the right time. You will make a ton of money doing this, if you can pull it off. Rarely do I see it work consistently. If you disagree take a look at this:

- "Bear Stearns Is Fine!" Jim Kramer, on his TV Show Mad Money, March 11, 2008

- "American consumers might benefit if lenders provided greater mortgage product alternatives to the traditional fixed-rate mortgage." Alan Greenspan February 2004.

- "Read my lips: NO NEW TAXES." George Bush, 1988.

I am not trying to criticize these people. All of them are very smart. I am merely trying to convey just how hard it is not only to be right but to be right at the right *time*. That's why I prefer option two:

2. **You can be in everything so you don't have to guess what The Next Big Thing is.** If your stocks shoot up and everything else flutters, you can sell some of the stock and spread it around the other investments, thereby taking your profits from The Next Big Thing (in this example, stocks) and betting on everything– gold, silver, real estate etc. – as The Next Big Thing. (Confused? Don't worry. This process is called *rebalancing* and is discussed in detail in Chapter 19.)

Unfortunately, what most people do is simply stand still and do nothing, much like I did with Charlotte and the worst pickup line of my life. This is probably the most dangerous option of all because it means leaving your money precisely where it is, and just watching as the economy changes. You might be wrong. Hell, the experts are wrong *most* of the time. But you can make adjustments, protect the downside and grab onto opportunities even when those opportunities began forming years ago.

The job of this book is to show you how.

You can always do something

Loser investments can only go to zero. Even the leveraged investments like real estate, if properly leveraged, can be sold for enough to pay the debt. But there is no limit on winning investments. If you are properly diversified, you won't get rich betting on the right side of the crash, but you'll do fine.

Part 2
The Boring Stuff

WARNING: ENTERING THE BORING CHAPTERS. THE FOOD AND DRUG ADMINISTRATION WARNS THE FOLLOWING CHAPTERS CAN CAUSE DROWSINESS, DIZZINESS, AND AN UNRELENTING DESIRE TO CHECK FACEBOOK.

Chapter 9

BANKING ON DISASTER

Everyone needs to save six to eight months worth of living expenses in an emergency account. If your car breaks down, if you lose your job, or if you failed to tell the insurance company that you changed from Gandolph the Grey to Gandolph the White, and they are now denying you coverage, you'll be glad you had this fund. Your emergency fund will prevent you from dipping into your retirement accounts, selling your house early, or making some other hasty and unwise financial decision.

Two questions should be percolating in your mind. One, how the flip are you supposed to save this much money? And two, where do you put it? Let's start with question #1.

No touching

You don't need to have all this money saved by tomorrow night. It will take months, maybe even a year or two. But the point is to get started and *not touch the money once it lands in the account*. The easiest way to do this is to set up some sort of automatic deduction from your existing bank account. Even better, ask your employer to send part of your paycheck to this account.

What you *don't* want to do is link this account to your current checking and savings accounts. For many people, "saving" is a five-step process:

Step 1: Deposit money into checking account.

Step 2: Move some of that money into savings account via the bank's website.

Step 3: When Friday night arrives, move money from savings account *back* into checking account.

Step 4: Party.

Step 5: Sunday morning, check balance, and curse "WTF did all my money go?"[27]

You have to set yourself up to win, and that means making it *difficult* to get at this emergency fund. Maybe that means opening up an online bank account and refusing the ATM card when they send it. Or opening the account at a bank that is a two-hour drive from your house. Anything that forces you to jump through a few hoops to get the money.

> Money that is easy to get is easy to spend.

Where to stash the cash:

People spend waaaaaaay to much time trying to find the ideal place to park their emergency fund. Indeed, you may gain an extra point of interest by shopping around, but it's more important to get the fund started than it is find the best deal. Still, I can offer a bit of advice when it comes to shopping for a super safe place to stash your cash, whether the account will be to pay everyday bills or for emergencies.

---

27   For the purposes of this book, the "W" in "WTF" might stand for "what", "where", or "why." The "T" will always stand for "the." The "F", well, you know.

- **Typically interest rates will be better with the online banks:** Online banks don't have to pay the expensive real estate costs associated with bank branches. So they can pass this savings onto you. Another benefit of online banks, at least for the emergency account, is that if you refuse to accept an ATM card, it can be difficult to get your money immediately. This is a good thing when it comes to your disaster fund. www.etrade.com and www.ally.com are two good places to start.

- **www.bankrate.com is constantly posting who has the best interest rates:** You can log on there to see who is on top. Keep in mind these change constantly, but it's a start.

- **Consider a credit union:** Credit unions are essentially non-profit banks. Rather than having "customers" credit unions have "members." When you open an account you become a member, which means you are entitled to some of the profits of the credit union. Instead, they distribute those profits by offering their members lower fees, free checking and better interest rates. Check out www.cuna.org and www.ncua.org for suggestions in your area.

- **A money market account will have a better interest rate:** The money market is a market just like the stock market, but instead of trading stocks, short-term debts are traded. Major corporations and governments always need short-term loans, and they go to the money market to get them. But whose money are they borrowing? Yours, when you open a money market account. Some money market accounts are not insured by the FDIC, which makes them slightly more risky.[28] Hence the better interest rate.

- **Relationships may be the most important thing in choosing a bank:** As I write this, the credit markets are tight. For the last decade, banks were rather loose with their money, and now they (or more likely *we*) are paying for it. Part of the reason we got into this mess is we relied too heavily on formulas (credit scores and credit reports) and not enough on personal relationships. So consider a bank - and it will most likely be a small bank or credit union - where you can create a relationship.

---

28   The FDIC is the Federal Deposit Insurance Corporation that protects the money in your bank accounts from theft and the bank itself going bankrupt.

You can always do something

Don't get too stressed out about where to park your short term cash or your emergency fund. Pick a place and get started. You can always change later. Set up a plan to have 10% of your paycheck sent to your emergency account until you have 6-8 months of living expenses saved.

Chapter 10

TAXES

Taxes suck.

Paying them sucks. Preparing them sucks. Paying someone to prepare them sucks. So it should be no illusion that reading about them will suck. I will do my best to make this as painless as possible.

The good news is that if I were to suggest a good time to pay for financial advice, taxes would be it. For most Americans, when you combine their sales, income, and property taxes with all the tiny taxes, like tollbooths and car registrations[29], taxes are the single biggest expense. So don't be afraid to pay for some help.

Don't tell me you don't make enough money to hire a tax advisor either. I used to work for one of the major retail tax franchises (not that one, the other one) and about 90% of my clients made less than $50,000 a year. Some were on welfare, and one was fresh out of prison (or recently escaped from prison, I can't remember which). The point is, I saw all sorts of clients of all sorts of income, many of whom made less money than you.[30]

Since tax laws change every year, and since I have no idea about your income, deductions, family status or even the state you live in, allow me to provide some general tax tips:

---

29 *Registration* is French for "tax."
30 Who was the most interesting client? A handsome Harvard man (yes, my office was right near Harvard) strolled in one morning with a form known as 1099-MISC, in which one declares miscellaneous income. The income source? Sperm donation. There was about a half-hour argument on where to file this income on the return, some arguing for schedule C, meaning he was self-employed and this was his, uhh, "business"; others argued for Line 21 on Form 1040, which is where you put the money you earned that doesn't fall anywhere else. Eventually Line 21 won out.

- **Earned money that comes into your pocket is taxed; an increase in net worth is not.** The money you earn from your job comes into your pocket every week or month and that money will be taxed. But if you bought 100 shares of MacDonald's stock at $50 and it is now $100, you will not be taxed on that income until you sell it, and it comes into your pocket. This may sound overly simple, but it is this strategy, *deferring* the money that comes into your pocket, that rich people use above any other. An employee earns money, pays his taxes, then pays his bills with the leftover money. A business owner earns money, pays her bills, *then* pays taxes with the money left over.

- **There are only three ways to reduce your taxes without cheating: 1) a tax deduction 2) a tax credit or 3) a tax shelter**

  - A **tax deduction** is an amount of money you can deduct from your taxable income. If you make $50,000 this year and you have a $10,000 tax deduction, you can subtract that amount, leaving you with only $40,000 in taxable income. Tax deductions are good, but they are not as good as tax credits.

  - **Tax credits** are an amount of money you can deduct *directly* from your taxes. So sticking with the example above, you first subtract $10,000 from your income, leaving taxable income of $40,000. Assume we live in a fantasy world where taxes are only 10%, so you are left with a tax bill of $4,000. Now let's crank up this fantasy and pretend you have a $1,500 tax credit. You could subtract that amount right off the $4,000 tax bill.

  - **Tax shelters** are not that common anymore. A simple example might be the popular retirement accounts like the 401k or Roth IRA, which allow your money to grow protected from taxes. Tax shelters are also the term given to more complicated strategies such as income shifting (getting paid in the next year, when you expect your taxes to be lower than in this year) and asset allocation into non taxable investments such as municipal bonds.

- **Typically the more you earn, the more you pay.** Our tax system is (or tries to be) progressive. A progressive tax system has several different tax rates, each one increasing as someone earns more. Imagine a simple world where tax rates were 10% on the first $10,000 in income, 20% on the next $10,000 income, and 30% on the next $10,000 in income. The first $10,000 of income you earned would be taxed at 10%. But earn just *one more* dollar and that additional dollar is taxed at 20%. If you earned $40,000, then your tax bill would be $9000. (10% on the first $10,000 or $1,000; 20% on the next $10,000 or $2,000; and 30% on the remaining $20,000 or $6,000.) The importance here is that a tiny tax deduction can be worth quite a bit if it brings your taxable income *down* into a lower tax bracket. There are a lot of folks whose incomes fall on the border, and it's that last $1,000 that hurts the most.

- **Ask for an *enrolled agent* if you use a retail tax firm like H&R Block, Tax Man or Jackson Hewitt.** An enrolled agent is a person who has passed an IRS exam and is able to represent you in an audit. They have a heightened level of tax knowledge and have passed a test to prove it. Despite this fact, the big retail tax firms do not charge more when your tax return is prepared by an enrolled agent. Bernie the Fossil, an enrolled agent who actually did Napoleon's taxes, will cost the same as Two Week Willy. So ask to work with an enrolled agent. You'll get ten times the experience for the same price.

- **Declare all income, but be aggressive on deductions:** It is widely held myth that the IRS cares about the *amount* of money you cheat. They don't. It's not okay to cheat a little under the guise of "They have bigger fish to fry." Indeed they do, but here's an interesting fact most people don't know: IRS agents are compensated not only on the *amount* of money they bring back from an audit, but also on the *number* of audits they do. So they are rewarded by frying a whole bunch of small fish just as much as they are from frying a big fish. What's more, big fish have expensive, sleazy lawyers to protect them. Most small fish do not. The simple way to avoid these problems is to declare all income. If you worked at that booth at the state fair and the guy paid you in cash, still declare it

(Because he might have deducted it from his income taxes, even though he paid you in cash.) If you have a quiet little quilting business on EBay, be sure you tell the IRS how much you netted from sewing.[31]

- **Always file a tax return, even if you hardly made anything at all.** When I worked for that giant tax franchise (no, not that one, the *other* one), it was 2001. One slow Tuesday morning, a gent walked in and said he was being audited by the IRS. "No problem," I told him, "we can certainly help. What year's tax return are they auditing?" "1982," he said. The man did not file a return in 1982, thinking it was unnecessary because he made almost no money. Indeed he *may* have been right, but how was he going to prove that now? In 1982 he probably thought he could save a few bucks by not filing and instead spent the money on Michael's Jackson's *Thriller* album. Nineteen years later, he had a big problem.

- **Adjust form W-4:** If you are an employee, your employer will send you a W-2 form at the end of the year telling you how much money you earned and how much money they took out for taxes and FICA payments. But Form W-4 is the form you fill out BE-FOUR your start working for a new company. This form allows you to determine how much money you want withheld from your paycheck. I've found, through experience, that often people who have cash flow programs have too much money withheld. HR can help you adjust this form.

- **Most important of all, get some help so you can focus on tax *strategy*, not just tax *preparation*.** Most people can summarize their tax strategy in two words: Oh S&^%! What I mean is, most people don't think about taxes until they are due, and usually even that is at the eleventh hour. They are simply trying to get their taxes *prepared*. It's a reactive strategy. If you want more money in your pocket, you need to think about a *proactive* strategy. Again, when I was working for that national tax chain (no, not that one) I helped many people with small incomes. Simple things like determining who should claim the child on their return (if the

---

31   And *certainly* tell them how much you lost if that was the case. You can deduct that against your ordinary income.

child spends half their time with each parent), and then having the claiming parent write the non claiming parent a check for the difference in the form of a tax-free gift, is a good example of how a simple strategy can save you money.[32]

You can always do something

Taxes are probably the single biggest expense in your life and with a 10 *million* word tax code, it's silly to go it alone. Get some help, but get that help in May, not in April. Plan out a whole year. Regardless of where the markets go, you need a tax strategy.

---

32 This is also a good example of a run-on sentence.

Chapter 11

INSURANCE

Insurance is, by far, the easiest part of a financial plan to ignore. After all, your everyday life doesn't change if you're rolling along without the proper insurance. In fact, your day to day life is probably *better*. All those other insured schleps have to spend a few hundred bucks a month on premiums, while you can spend that money on dinners, drinks, donuts, and dodgeball tournaments. This is all well and good until you get hit by a bus.

It needn't be a big bus. It actually doesn't need to be a bus at all. Your "bus" could be a tree falling on your car, a pipe bursting in your apartment, a thief breaking into your house, or a common cold that gets frighteningly nasty. As the old saying goes, "It's all fun and games until someone loses an eye."

All insurance policies have four basic parts:

- **The premium:** This is what you pay.

- **The coverage:** This is what you get.

- **The deductible:** This is what you cough up before the coverage kicks in. If your car insurance policy has a $500 deductible, and you crash into Optimus Prime as he is chasing Megatron through the streets of New York, the first $500 in damage to your car (or Optimus Prime's right leg) are paid for by you. Above that, your coverage takes over.

- **The riders:** Not all policies have riders. Many that don't however, should. A rider is an add-on to an insurance policy that provides coverage not included in the standard policy. For instance, most homeowner's policies cover you if your house burns in a fire, but many offer *no* protection against earthquakes. Earthquake protection usually comes in the form of a rider. In additional to increasing *what* is covered, riders can also increase how much is covered. If your house burns to the ground, your $10 million original Da Vinci painting will probably go with it. If you had such a painting, you should probably add a rider to increase your insurance coverage above $10 million, to cover the painting.[33]

Gotcha covered

When I ask people about their insurance many will claim, "I'm covered." The real answer should be, "I'm covered for some stuff, up to a limit." A person with a homeowner's insurance policy may be covered for fire but not flood, and the fire may only cover $300,000, even though the cost to replace the house and all the stuff in it is more like $450,000.

Before we get to what insurance you need and how much of it, let's go over a few insurance rules of thumb.

- **Buy big policies and use riders:** I don't mean expensive or excessive policies. Rather, it is better to buy a policy on your house, and then cover all the little stuff with riders, than it is to buy a bunch of individual policies. Here's an example. Since identity theft is the fastest growing crime in the world, many companies (banks, credit card companies, and even identity theft protection companies) are offering identity theft insurance. For a small payment of $10 or so per month, you can get this insurance. If your bank accounts are hacked, these companies will immediately send you $2,000 to cover expenses until you get your life back. And if a criminal steals money that is not recoverable, these companies will send you a check for the money you have lost. Sounds good and $10 a month isn't that much right? Right! Except most homeowners insurance policies will offer the *same* protection for as little as $25 a *year.*

---

33 Interestingly enough, the Mona Lisa is actually *not* insured. Curators realized the cost of the insurance would be better spent on increased security.

- **Forget the "only if" policies:** An "only if" policy covers you "only if" X happens. If, and only if, you die in an airplane crash, your family gets the life insurance. But if you die on the way to the airport in a cab, or have a heart attack in the security line, or choke to death on your ninth Cinnabon at the food court, you are not covered. Statistically speaking, "only if" policies are a rip off. Better to have a comprehensive insurance policy that covers you regardless of the cause.

- **Be aware of the exclusions:** While comprehensive policies are preferred over "only if" policies, many of the all inclusive policies still have exclusions. In the world of life insurance, for example, there are restrictions on suicide and dying while involved in an illegal activity, such as drunk driving. There may be exclusions on high-risk activities like skydiving. A very simple insurance question to ask is, "What's not covered in this policy?"

> A very simple insurance question to ask is, "What's not covered in this policy?"

- **Constantly shop around:** "Could switching to Geico really save you 15% of more on car insurance?" It could, so be sure to try. Here's another question to ask. "Could switching *away from* Geico really save you 15% or more in car insurance?" The answer to that is "yes" as well. A good rule of thumb is to shop around for *all* of your insurance policies (except life and disability) at least once every two years. Geico could be the best deal this year, but

Progressive might win next year, and Allstate the year after that. Loyalty is dead in the insurance world, so don't be afraid to switch.

- **Beware of overlapping:** Often an employee with health insurance has at least *some* life and disability insurance in their benefits package. Members of associations, unions, or alumni groups often get a bit of insurance just for being members. Even some credit cards offer perks, like rental car insurance, to their members. Don't buy the same coverage twice.

- **Look for the break point:** The break point, in insurance terms, is the point at which it no longer makes economic sense to increase the deductible. Suppose for instance that on your auto insurance a $500 deductible yields a policy that costs $1,000 a year. But by accepting a $1,000 deductible you can drop those premiums to $600 a year. The money you save in the first year alone is nearly worth it. Excited at this savings, you press the insurance salesperson for more. "Suppose," you say, "I go to a $2,000 deductible?" The salesperson types a suspicious number of keyboard keys and responds, "That would drop the premiums to $550 a year." Ladies and gentlemen, we have found the break point. Agreeing to take on another $1,000 in your deductible doesn't seem to save you that much.[34]

So those are some rules of thumb to look for when purchasing any insurance policy. The question now is what insurance policies do you need? Depending on where you live, be it in your own home or one you rent, you'll need six out of the seven types of insurance. Let's start with the one everyone skips:

Disability: Disability insurance is sometimes referred to as income insurance. It pays you a salary if you are no longer able to do your job. If you are hit by a bus, health insurance will pay the medical bills for you to recover. But once you are out of the hospital, you still have two broken legs and a broken arm, so you cannot do your ice road trucker job. Disability would pay you an income, about 60%-80% of your current salary, until you recover.

---

34   The odd thing about this strategy is how few insurance people actually use it. They often give blanket quotes, not even caring that with just a little bit more deductible you, their customer, could save a bundle.

Most people live under the illusion that their employer offers disability insurance. Often they offer some coverage, but not enough. Most businesses and nonprofits will cover you for 60 days, while the average disability lasts much longer – sometimes even the rest of your life. So you may need a disability policy that builds on to the one your company offers.[35] Ideally you want a policy that pays 60%-80% of your income until you turn 65 years old, when Social Security will (hopefully) kick in. You cannot get a policy that covers 100% of your income; that makes it too tempting to become, wink wink, "disabled."

The price of a disability policy is affected by five things: your age, your health, your job, the income you want to replace, and the length of time that passes before the policy kicks in. This last item is considered the deductible on a disability policy. If you can wait 6 months before receiving checks, either by living off your employer's policy or living off your savings, you will drastically save over the person who begins getting checks right away. Obviously the younger you are, the healthier you are, the smaller your income and the safer your job, the cheaper your policy will be. But it is crucial to get *something*.

Start by asking your employer what, if anything, is currently offered. Build on that. If there's nothing, consider joining a professional association to see if they have a group policy. Remember the longer you wait with disability the more it will cost you, literally. For a complete questionnaire on what to ask when shopping for a disability policy, please visit the Resources section of my website www.peterbielagus.com.

Life: Life insurance pays a lump sum of money when you die to the person you designate, a.k.a. the beneficiary. The purpose of it is to replace your salary since you are not really an effective worker, being dead and all. There are two types of life insurance: *term* and *whole life*.

Term, as the name states, lasts for only a certain term. You may be covered for 10 years, 20 years, or 30 years. Die within the term, and your policy pays out. Die one day after the term, and your heirs get nothing. Whole life differs in three primary ways. The first is that it lasts your whole life. As long as you pay the premiums, you are covered. The second is that whole life builds up a cash value, one that earns interest, much

---

35   BTW, the world's second most famous duck (after Daffy) is the AFLAC duck. AFLAC is a company that sells disability policies that add onto your employer's policy (And no, I don't work for AFLAC).

like a bank account. And the third is, because of differences one and two, whole life is more expensive, on average about ten times the price of term. The simplest advice, one that most personal finance authors, including myself, suggest, is to buy term insurance and invest the money you save elsewhere. On the surface, this is solid advice, but it does have three serious flaws:

1. It sounds like a good idea, but many people don't invest the difference they save by buying term. Instead they spend it on flat screen TVs and burritos.

2. The second is that after about 25 years, term starts to get more expensive than whole life, especially considering that whole life is building up a cash reserve.

3. For many people, once their term policies expire, they cannot get them renewed. If you had a bout with cancer, even a successful one, forget it. Diabetes too can make the cost of renewing a term policy prohibitive.

That is not to say that the whole life champions are correct either. Most whole life policies are fat with commissions. The reason the top financial authors despise them is because they can be extremely confusing, and if you cancel them in the first five years you end up losing around 70% of the money you put in. Often the single mom is sucker punched into buying a whole life policy, only to discover she cannot keep up with the payments for more than a year or two. There are even some policies, known as variable life, that can cannibalize themselves if interest rates or the stock market go the wrong way.

When it comes to shopping for life insurance, it's tempting to do nothing rather than sort through the sea of policies. But this book is all about fighting the desire to do nothing, so here is what I suggest:

- **Don't look for the right policy, look for the right salesperson.** The same policy can be bought at the same company but from two different life insurance agents and be drastically different in terms of the commissions taken out. Ask friends and family who they recommend, but find that person who wants to set up a long-term relationship with *you* and not just with your wallet.

- **Have this person run all the numbers, whether they want to or not.** (And if they don't want to run the numbers, you are working with the wrong person.) Here is what I mean by running the numbers. Supposed you are a 29-year-old unmarried person with no children. Right now you don't really need life insurance. But if you are pretty certain marriage and kids are in your future, then you will need it at some point and it may be cheaper in the long run to buy it now. The reason is because the price of insurance is based on your health and age *today*. Should you get diabetes in two years, the price will skyrocket. It may also skyrocket after your 30th birthday. So ask your life insurance agent:

    - *What would a 30-year, level term policy of X amount cost me now?*

    - *What would a whole life policy of that same amount cost me now?*

    - *What would these policies cost if I waited five years to buy them?*

    - *If I did buy the whole life, how does its true cost, including premiums and the built up cash value, compare against the term policy? Please use only the guaranteed dividend rates.*

Keep pounding away until you have the comparisons you need to make a decision.

- **In the case of whole life, don't let the life insurance salesperson use the best case numbers.** Only accept the worst case numbers. These are the guaranteed numbers and they can be found on the *left side* of any chart the salesperson slides in front of you. The good news (which he'll keep pointing to) is on the right. Ignore that.

- **If you do buy term, you'll want a 20- to 30-year level premium term policy.** This means the premiums will not go up during the term of the policy. Twenty years is usually an affordable number, but often thirty is cost prohibitive. Again, force your life insurance agent to run the numbers.

- **Auto and Home:** Since most people buy a car and a house with some sort of loan, a lot of the insurance guesswork is done for you. The lender will have certain standards the policy must meet, because if the house burns to the ground or your car is totaled, they want to be sure their investment is protected. But don't forget to ask, "What is *not* covered in my policy?" Your bank may not require earthquake insurance for your house, since it is so rare in your area. If however, your house is destroyed by one, you are on the hook. Also nowhere else in the insurance world will you discover the benefits of shopping around than with auto and home policies.

Health: 'Tis this insurance that has, for a very long time, stirred a nationwide debate. If your employer covers you, you are in luck. If they don't, then you are not necessarily out of luck. There are two types of affordable health insurance policies for those who do not have it through their employer:

- **Temporary insurance:** Is just that, it goes away after a certain time period. These policies usually last about six months, and most states allow you to renew them for up to a total of 18 months. Because the insurance company will only be on the hook for so long, these policies are drastically cheaper. What's more, once you have one, you slide under the ominous "pre-existing condition" radar, so when you do go to get a permanent policy, they cannot deny you.[36]

- **Catastrophe insurance:** Remember how you can lower your premiums by taking a larger deductible? Catastrophe insurance takes this to the extreme with a very large deductible, of say $10,000-$15,000. While this is not ideal coverage, it is better than nothing. Premiums for these policies can be 70 percent off what normal insurance is.

Uninsured injuries are the number one reason people declare personal bankruptcy. So despite the cost and all the frustrations surrounding health insurance, try as best you can to get *something*.

---

36 There are of course proposals in Congress to get rid of the pre-existing condition rules altogether, but this will most likely be a nasty drawn out fight. Perhaps by the time you read this, it will be all sorted out. But I doubt it.

Renters: If you rent your home instead of own it, you need renter's insurance. Renter's is the one form of insurance I will accept no arguments for. It's cheap. It costs less than $200 a *year*. This insurance protects the stuff in your apartment, and it even protects that stuff when it leaves your apartment. If your skis are stolen out of your car, renter's would cover that. If a pipe bursts and all your stuff is ruined, the landlord may not have to pay for it. And if your drunk friend falls down your steps and sues you[37] your landlord definitely does not have to pay for that. For the price of a pizza or two, you can, and should, get renter's insurance.

Umbrella: An umbrella policy is an insurance policy on your insurance policies. Basically if you get sued, say from a car accident that was your fault - you were warned not to text - then your car insurance company would pay for the legal defense and if necessary pay the award settlement. The trouble is, insurance policies have a cap on the protection. If your car insurance policy has a $500,000 limit, then *you* are responsible if the opposing team sues you for more than that. That is to say, you're responsible if you *don't* have an umbrella policy. If you did, the umbrella would kick in once the other policies ran out of steam. People with any amount of impressive assets (say, a house or a business) should consider an umbrella policy. They're pretty affordable, around $300 a year for most folks, and they can help you breathe easier.

For more great strategies to consider when purchasing insurance, please visit the Resources section of my website at www.peterbielagus.com

---

You can always do something

It doesn't matter where the stock market, unemployment numbers or political elections end up. *You need insurance.* Without insurance, you have no financial plan at all. Spending five minutes on insurance will improve your financial life far more than spending five hours researching stocks.

---

37   Some friend!

Chapter 12

CREDIT

Credit is a measure of people's faith in you, at least in a financial sense. People with good credit will have an easier time getting a loan, insurance, a cell phone, and cable TV. Good credit can help people rent an apartment, even get a job.

Credit is measured using two tools: a *credit report* and a *credit score*. The credit report is nothing more than a history of how well you have paid your bills, how well you have handled the money lent to you, and how aggressively you have tried to borrow money. The credit score is simply the numeric summary of a credit report. When you do something dumb, your score goes down. When you do something smart, your score goes up. Well I should say, what *they* think is dumb and smart.

The trouble is, companies have the right to report *only* the dumb things you do and never give you credit for any of the smart things.[38] You could pay your rent on time for seven years straight without your landlord ever reporting it on your credit report. But that one time, that *one time* you went a little too crazy at the Vegas Bachelorette party, resulting in a 30-day late rent payment, your landlord phones you in.

Who does he phone BTW? He phones one, or all three, of the major credit reporting agencies. The three titans – Experian, Transunion and Equifax – dominate the credit reporting world. These companies (referred to as "The Big Three") handle about 80% of the credit reports in the United States. Whenever you sign up for a cell phone, get another student loan, finance a car, or put a mortgage on your house, somewhere, in that

---

38   I feel I get this same treatment in my relationships.

fine print that no one ever reads, the cell phone/student loan/auto dealer/ mortgage company demands the right to report your payment history to the credit bureaus. When you pay on time, these companies send a message to the credit reporting agencies saying, "Kim paid her mortgage on time this month."[39] When you pay late, they send that information, too.

The Big Three compile this data onto your credit report because it serves as a tool to predict how likely you will pay your bills on time. In this world, the past *does* equal the future. Bureaus believe that what you did yesterday is a pretty good reflection of what you are going to do tomorrow. They are not the only ones. Millions of companies, from all sorts of industries, use credit reports to predict what you are going to do next.

Before a landlord hands over the keys, he will check your credit report. Before the auto dealer hands over the keys, she will check your credit. Before the mortgage company hands over the keys, they will check your credit. And if you were to borrow money from Alicia Keys, she would want to check your credit report. The good news is that no one can pull your credit report without your permission. The bad news is that in order to get the loan, car or apartment, you *have* to give them your permission.

A wee bit of history...

Credit reports were actually created in the late 1800s. Stores would let people buy stuff on credit and would keep handwritten records on those people. When a person wanted more credit for another purchase, storeowners would refer to what they wrote down earlier.[40] Then, in the 1950s along came two guys who had WAY too much free time and probably no girlfriends. Bill Fair (an engineer) and Earl Isaac (a mathematician) argued they could create a mathematical formula that could *read* a credit report better than an individual.

Isaac and Fair began analyzing thousands of credit reports and began to see trends. They noticed when someone paid late one month, they were more likely to pay late next month. When someone applied for a new loan, they too were more likely to pay late. The gents began assigning and deducting points to these trends, and the FICO Score was born.

---

39 Assuming of course, your name is Kim.
40 I always wondered, "What if they had sloppy handwriting?"

Named after its founders, the Fair Isaac Company (FICO) score is still the most popular credit score in the world. Based on a scale of 300 (the worst) to 850 (the best), it summarizes all the data on the credit report. If your score is good enough, loans, cell phones and apartments easily come your way. If not, then you must fight, argue and eventually pay more for all those things.

At the time of this writing, most lenders would consider a score of 750 or better to be an "A" credit score. Above 750 is pretty much bragging rights. People with scores below this number can still get credit, but "A" credit means you get the best deal available for the product or service at hand. Based on current rates, an A credit borrower might get a car loan at 5%, a B credit person (somewhere between 749-650) might get that same loan at 6%. C credit (649-550) is probably looking at 7-9% for that car loan, D credit (549-450) will get pummeled with a loan around 12%, and F credit (below 450) probably couldn't get a car loan, and even if they could, they should probably just take the bus.

So that's the history. If I have done my job, two questions should be floating in your mind right now:

1. What does my credit report and score look like?

2. How can I improve them?

You can start by turning the page.

You can always do something

Like insurance, credit scores and reports are something you can focus on to improve your financial life regardless of where the market goes. Keep reading to find out what you can do.

Chapter 13

CREDIT REPORTS AND SCORES

As of the date of this writing, there are two places I recommend to check your score. One won't ever change, the other one might. The websites are:

- www.annualcreditreport.com
- www.creditkarma.com

For years (about 50), credit reporting agencies had a serious problem they didn't want anyone to know about: They never had a system in place to double check credit reports. For example, if your credit report said you had 30 open cell phone accounts, which is a bit silly, there was no guy sitting in a cubicle in Cincinnati flipping through binders of credit reports, dog earing corners of the unusual ones. There was nothing.

Fun Fact: A company called E Loan was actually the first company to allow their customers to see their own credit scores.

In fairness to the credit reporting agencies, creating a double check system is not easy. Even if they did have a guy in Cincinnati double checking reports, it would be rather tedious to flip through the 100 million of them in existence. In a rare moment of brilliance, Congress found the solution: *you double check*. In 2003, they passed the Fair and Accurate Credit Transactions Act (FACT Act), which, among other things, forced the Big Three to give you a free copy of your credit reports, once per year. To accommodate the new law, the Big Three established www.annualcreditreport.com. It is the *only* site that is truly nonprofit. They do not sell anything and they don't even ask for your email address. It's a great site.

Except for one thing: You cannot get your score for free. If you want that you will have to pay, somewhere in the neighborhood of $8 per score. That's the bad news.

The good news is that as of the time of this writing, there is another website that will not only give you your credit report for free, it will also give you your credit score for free. www.creditkarma.com is a for-profit website, mind you, but currently they make money off advertising and up selling. If you don't buy anything, you can still get your report and score for free.

Fun Fact: While the FICO score (300-850) is the most widely used credit score in the world with about 70% of all professional lenders using it, it is hardly alone. There are more than *100* different scores, so it can be tough to do an apples-to-apples comparison.

What am I looking for?

As you look over your credit reports, you are basically asking yourself one question:

Do I agree with this?

Whether your report reads good news or bad news, the most important thing is that the report is accurate. If you see something that does not make sense, there will be a button next to each item on your report that reads "dispute this item."[41] Click on this button and you can fill out a form to dispute the item. Hit send and then that dispute form zips to the credit bureaus.

From here, it's their problem and they have 30 days to get back to you proving that it is your mistake. If they cannot, they have to take it off the report. Easy.

Well ...

While the law states it is supposed to move like clockwork it often doesn't. I've seen far too many disputes come back with the simple retort: "We have investigated your dispute and found the information on the report to be accurate." And that's it. Often the credit reporting agency calls the lender who reported the late payment. The lender then checks their records, and sure enough, you were late (because computers are never wrong).

Many times you have to push back harder. According to the Fair Credit Reporting Act, § 611 Paragraph (6)(b)(iii), the credit reporting agency must furnish you *"with a description of the procedure used to determine the accuracy and completeness of the information shall be provided to the consumer by the agency, including the business name and address of any furnisher of information contacted in connection with such information and the telephone number of such furnisher"*.

In short, while they often send you just a quick email response, you can request to know the complete results of the investigation. But they _don't_ have to give this information automatically. You have to ask the credit reporting agency for it. And often this gets the issue cleared up.

---

41   Or at least this is what it says on annualcreditreport.com. I can't speak for all the other sites, but this is the one you should be going to anyway.

Up until this point, the burden of proof has been on *them*. It's not your job to prove you didn't, it is their job to prove you did. But if the mistake is still on there, and you have the written proof in your hand (a cleared check, a paid receipt, whatever) it's time you contacted *both* the credit reporting agencies (all three) *and* the company that put the mistake on your report (American Express, Visa, GMAC, etc.). Send everyone your proof reminding them they need to take it off the report.

If you don't get a response, send another letter threatening to report them to both the attorney general of their state and the Federal Trade Commission. Still no response, then send those letters and copy the companies in on them. Don't want to write the letters? Don't worry. I wrote them for you. They can be found on my website (www.peterbielagus. com) under the Resources section.

Credit reports – and fixing the inherent errors within – are one of the most popular sections of my speeches. I run into countless audience members who have been fighting with the credit reporting agencies and with collection agents to get errors removed. They ask for my help. "No problem," I say, "just email me the paperwork you've sent them so far." A frown begins to form. An eyebrow is raised. "Paperwork?" they say, "I've been doing it all over the phone."

When it comes to getting errors removed off of your credit report, you win the war with paper. If you don't have a paper trail, you need to start at the beginning and go from there. Unfortunately, this process is something you need to do every year for the rest of your life, as mistakes can pop up at anytime.[42]

And the score is:

The first thing to know about credit scores is what they are made up of. A credit score is essentially the outcome of running your credit report through an algorithm. The formula assigns points for certain things and takes away points for others. Every time you check your score, the computer takes your credit report, runs it through the algorithm, and then spits out a score.

---

42   Hence the reason it is called "annualcreditreport.com" and not "once-in-a-while-assuming-I-have-some-free-time-and-nothing-cool-is-on-TV-creditreport.com."

While there are several different types of scores, for the purposes of this chapter, I am going to be outlining mainly what makes up the FICO score. Remember, however, that most credit scores follow the same general guidelines. The FICO score looks at five areas on your credit report:

1. **Payment history:** This is the single biggest factor considered. It counts for 35% of your score. There is *nothing* more important in the world of credit scoring than paying your bills on time.

2. **Amounts owed:** Put simply, the more debt you have, the lower your score. Except, it is not that simple, so more on this a minute.

3. **Length of history:** The score not only cares about how well you have been doing with your payments, it also cares about how *long* you have been doing well.

4. **New credit:** The credit score keeps an eye on every time you apply for new credit.

5. **Types of credit used:** The score likes to see diversification. If you pay your credit card on time, it's impressed. But if you pay your credit card *and* your student loans on time, it's even more impressed.

So that's what's in a score. But it's just as important to know what's *not* in your credit score:

- **How much money you make:** The score doesn't care. You could be unemployed for that matter. The *lender* will care whether or not you have an income, but the score does not look at that.

- **How much money you have in the bank:** Again the lender might care about this one, but like income, it does not show up in the credit score calculation.

- **Your age:** Doesn't care. Young people do tend to have lower credit scores, but this simply has to do with length of history. If a 90-year-old man just started building his credit yesterday, his score would suck.

- **Your race, color, creed, sex etc.:** None of this is on the report.

- **Where you live:** Doesn't matter.[43]

- **What your spouse's score is:** Contrary to popular belief, when you get married, you do not get a merged credit score. You will always have yours, and your better half will always have theirs. If you were to buy a house together and sign jointly on a loan, the banker would average your credit scores together, creating, ipso facto, a "merged" score. But this could be done whenever two people sign a loan – father and son, two business partners, anyone. There is no such thing as a merged credit report.

- **Whether or not you are participating in credit counseling of any kind:** Thankfully they got rid of this one.

- **Anything that is not on your credit report:** Simple but true; if it is not on your credit report, it cannot be factored into your credit score.

So now that you know what makes up your score, here is what makes it go up and down:

On the down low:

- **Paying late:** As stated above, nothing hurts your score more than a late payment. The good news is that in the world of credit scores, "late" is typically referred to as more than 30 days late. Some companies don't even bother to report you unless you are at least 60 days late. Of course, this is not an excuse to avoid paying on time, because companies pummel you with late fees if you are so much as a day overdue.

- **Letting your credit be pulled:** Every time your credit is checked, it's referred to as an *inquiry.* There are two types of inquiries.[44] A *soft inquiry* occurs when you check your credit for informational purposes only, like a visit to annualcreditreport.com. This doesn't

---

43 A common misconception occurs here because people in certain areas of the country "seem" to get better interest rates. This has nothing to do with credit scores and has everything to do with the cost to banks of lending money. It is cheaper, typically, for a bank to lend money in rural Mississippi than in Los Angeles. Real estate is cheaper and labor is cheaper, so there will typically be a lower interest rate in Mississippi on say, a home loan, than in the expensive city of Los Angeles.

44 Okay fine. There is a third type of inquiry, the *promotional inquiry.* Thankfully it does not hurt your score. This one gives companies the right to pull a limited version of your credit report to offer you more credit. Ya know, those preapproved credit card offers? All from promotion inquiries. You can stop them at www.optoutprescreen.com.

hurt your score. A *hard inquiry* however, does. These occur when you let someone pull your credit because you are attempting to borrow more money. The catch is that sometimes a hard inquiry occurs even when you don't intend to borrow. Car dealers will often pull your credit before they let you test drive a car. Even worse, some don't want to talk to you until they know you can afford the car, and the only way they'll know is to pull your credit. That's why I suggest you print out a copy of your credit report so you can prove you are credit worthy without getting your report pulled all over town.

- **Doing nothing:** Your credit score is like a muscle, if you do nothing, over time it gets weaker. The payment history rewards you with "activity" so it can be important to have some payments on there to keep the score up. (More on how to do this in a minute.)

- **Borrowing a lot of money:** The score gets nervous when you have an above average amount of debt. "Average" is anyone's guess, but the score figures, and correctly so, that a person with a lot of debt will have more trouble making their next payment on time, than the person with little or no debt.

- **Screwing up your debt utilization ratios:** A *debt utilization ratio* is a measure of how much you did borrow against how much you can borrow. If your credit card has a $1,000 limit and you borrowed $500, then you have a 50% debt utilization ratio. The higher this ratio is, the closer you are to being "maxed out," and the lower your score will go.

- **Canceling a credit card:** This one really pisses me off, but it is true. When you cancel a credit card, that account, or "trade line," becomes inactive. Inactive accounts don't help your score as much as active ones (even if the payment history was a bit sloppy). If you do want to cancel a card or cards, consider canceling the youngest cards first or considering not using a card at all for a long period of time before canceling it.

On the upside:

- **Paying on time:** Nothing will help your score more than this. If you are going to be late, especially more than 30 days late, call your credit card company and tell them you are going to be late, and hopefully set up an automatic withdrawal for the date you expect you can pay. Often when you do this, they don't mark it as a late payment.

- **Fixing mistakes that are not your fault:** Why be punished for something you didn't do? Yet, *millions* of Americans are doing just that, so be sure to take an active step to fix your credit.

- **Keeping those debt utilization ratios low:** Try not to borrow more than 30% of your limit, especially *six months* before applying for a loan.

- **Having activity:** Unfortunately, people with no debts to pay actually suffer from lousy credit scores. This is silly, but the score does need *something* to latch onto, and those who never use credit cannot provide this. Consider having just one credit card and using it just once a month for a very small purchase that you can pay off every month. If credit cards outright terrify you, there is a way around this, which I'll discuss in the next chapter.

- **Keep at it:** The credit score is not impressed when you pay on time once. But do it consistently and you'll get rewarded. You get a "bonus" once you have been doing something well for two years in a row. And the longer you do something well, the more your score will rise.

You can always do something

If you consistently avoid the things that bring your score down, and cater to the things that bring your score up, you'll do fine. A great credit score will allow you to pay less for insurance, apartments, cell phones, homes, cars, college, even gym memberships. So be sure to check your report and score at least once a year. Currently have a terrible score? Then turn the page.

Chapter 14

BUILDING BACK UP YOUR CREDIT SCORE

Given enough time and enough of the previously discussed good behavior, all lousy credit scores can become great. By "enough time" I typically mean two to three years. This is because the credit scoring formula puts more weight on the recent stuff than on the old stuff. A late payment last week hurts far more than a late payment five years ago.

Your credit history spans seven years. If you do something dumb tomorrow, it will remain on your credit report for seven years until it drops off. There are a few things that remain on longer, such as personal bankruptcies, which stay on for ten years. And there are a few things that remain on for only a short period of time, such as hard inquiries, which remain on for two years.

Since the score counts most heavily what happened in the last two to three years, simply by waiting for the bad news on your report to get older, your score will go up. I often say, "You are never more than three years away from a great credit score." Now you know why.

Still, three years is a long time. So here are some things you can do to get your score up in a hurry.

- **Explain yourself:** By law, you can attach a 100-word statement to your credit reports that says anything you want. You could proclaim, "I love Justin Bieber" if you wanted to.[45] While the statement will not raise or lower your score, it shows you are on top of whatever credit problems you have. This can be reassuring to the lender reading your report. So if you have a bunch of late payments because you got laid off in 2009, put that in your statement.

---

45   But don't.

- **Use a credit card once a month:** Remember the score likes to see activity. Using a card once a month and paying it off won't cost you anything in interest and it will raise your score.[46] Of course, credit cards make many people nervous, so if you want to build your score without one, keep reading.

- **Get a micro loan:** A micro loan is a very tiny loan of less than $500. You get it by putting $500 into a bank account. Immediately the bank gives you a loan for $500. The bank pays off your loan with the $500 you deposited with them. Simple for you, super safe for the bank. And it builds your credit. Most big banks won't do these, but small banks and credit unions will.

- **Get a Good Will Adjustment:** Ahhh. Very few people know about this one. A Good Will Adjustment is a form of forgiveness from a creditor. If you normally pay on time, but had one screw up, you can ask for this. By law, the creditor does not have to give it to you, but if you are a loyal customer who usually pays on time, you have a good shot. When you call customer service (remember call the original creditor, not the credit reporting agency) you may have to talk to a supervisor or even the supervisor's supervisor. But it's worth a try. If you get it, it simply means the creditor reports the late payment as being paid on time.

- **Consider a pay for deletion contract:** Ahh, no one knows about this one either. Suppose you had medical insurance and got hurt. You went to the hospital, got cured and got out. Three months later a collection agent calls you and says you owe the hospital $200. "But I have insurance." you say. "You do," agrees the collection agent, "but it did not cover the cost of your crutches." You hang up, call your insurance company, and after being on hold for two days, you discover that indeed, crutches are not covered. Your insurance paid everything else but not that. So you owe the hospital. But now you are three months late. Your account has been turned over to a collection agent. Your score took a big hit because of this. What can be done? You guessed it, a pay for

---

46   There is a nasty rumor going around that you only get points on the score if you carry a balance. People claim you must pay some interest every month to raise your score. It's simply not true. The credit scoring formula does not care about paying interest; it cares about activity. If you charge something every month and pay it off in full, your score will go up.

deletion contract. A pay for deletion contract is used for situations like the above, where things just got F'd up, and it really was no one's fault. It is true that a creditor cannot report false information on your credit report.[47] But a creditor can choose *not to report at all.* With a pay for deletion contract, you agree to pay the creditor a certain amount, and they choose not to report the mistake to the credit bureaus. Where do you get a pay for deletion contract? The same place you get all your important financial information, in the Resources section of my website (www.peterbielagus.com).

- **Build your own credit report:** There are about 20 million Americans who live "off the grid," which means they use no credit whatsoever. Unfortunately these people can have a tough time getting a loan or renting an apartment. But contrary to popular belief, you can build your own credit report by collecting your on time statements from the bills you do pay. If you pay rent, cable, cell phone, electric bills and the like, get a letter from each company stating how long you have had an account and how well you have been paying. Put these in a file. Smaller banks will accept these for car and even home loans. It will take some convincing, but it is possible.

- **Avoid using a credit repair firm:** This industry exploded overnight and also sort of collapsed overnight. Once individuals were allowed to access their own credit reports, they realized just how many errors there were. So these firms sprang up to help. The two problems with these firms were A) they charged a fee to do many things you could do on your own for free (like dispute errors) and B) they did some illegal things, like frivolous disputing and trying to get you a new Social Security Number. So steer clear and do it yourself.

---

47   The Good Will Adjustment being the rare exception to this, because technically in granting one, a creditor is saying you *did* pay on time, when in fact you did not.

- **Understand the score card system:** Okay, almost *no one* knows about this one, but this explains some of the weird stuff that happens when it comes to credit scores. I don't want to get into it here, since it cannot be used to raise your score, it will only explain the weird activity that sometimes happens. Visit the Resources section of my website (www.peterbielagus.com) to learn more.

You can always do something

I believe that almost anyone can get a great score in two to three years. When that starts is up to you. If your are curious, I have seen scores go up 200 points in one year. More questions and answers about debt consolidation plans, declaring bankruptcy, or the statute of limitations in your state, can be found in Resources section of my website (www.peterbielagus.com).

Chapter 15

RETIREMENT ACCOUNTS

I won't spend too much time on retirement accounts because they are boring, and I am trying to keep the boring part of this book as short as possible. But they deserve at least a few words because one of the most common (and most effective) ways to lower your tax bill is to do the bulk of your investing through a retirement account.

These accounts are essentially a bribe from the federal government. "Invest for your own retirement," says Uncle Sam, "and I'll give you a tax break." Uncle Sam defines "retirement" as age 59½. The money must remain in that account until you reach that age or there are tax penalties.[48]

Remember, too, that these are *accounts* that hold our investments. They are not investments in themselves. You put cash in them, and with that cash you purchase investments. Do all this inside the plan and your profits will be protected from taxes.

There are two types of retirement accounts:

1. Those sponsored by you

2. Those sponsored by your employer

If you haven't already, take a suspiciously long lunch break tomorrow and stroll down to the human resources department of your company. If your company is too small to have a human resources department, let alone the room to actually stroll, ask your boss about how the retirement

---

48   But don't let the tax penalties scare you because A) there are exceptions to getting your money out, and your tax advisor (since you now have one) can tell you what those are, and B) after your money has been in the account at least five years, the penalties don't hurt nearly as much when compared to what you have earned from money growing free from taxes.

accounts work. She may direct you to an 800 number, on the other end of which will be 15 minutes of elevator music.

But at the end of that elevator music will be a plan administrator. This guy will be able to tell you all about your company's retirement plan and how it works. He'll tell you what you can invest in. He can explain the tax advantages of the plan. He'll have graphs and charts and brochures and cool online calculators.

Before you determine which investments you should put inside your retirement account, you should first determine *which* type of account to get. Be it an employer sponsored plan or a individual sponsored plan, retirement accounts can be divided again into one of two categories:

1. Accounts that have the word "Roth" in their title

2. Accounts that don't have the word "Roth" in their title.

If an account has the word "Roth" in it, you can thank Senator William Roth, the dude who invented it. Accounts that bear his name *give you a tax break later*. Accounts that do not bear his name give you a *tax break now*.

Once money is inside a retirement account - any retirement account - it grows without the concern of taxes. Normally when you sell an investment at a profit, you must pay a tax on that profit. If an investment earns a dividend or interest, that income is also typically taxable the moment you receive it. Not so inside a retirement account. Your money grows faster when you don't have to pay taxes on it all the time.

But you do have to pay taxes *sometime*. Non-Roth accounts allow you to take a tax deduction the moment you put money into the account. So if you are in the 30% tax bracket, and you put $1,000 into your *non-Roth* retirement account, you can deduct $300 (30% of $1,000) off your taxes that year. That's the cool part. The catch is that when you turn 59½ and start taking money out, the money you withdrawal will be taxed as income.

So you get a tax break *now* as opposed to later.

Roth accounts are the opposite. You *cannot* take a tax deduction for putting money in. But when you begin withdrawing money at age 59½, that money is *not taxed at all*. With Roth accounts, you get the tax break *later* as opposed to now.

We could go through all the worksheets and calculators, but for most people, the Roth is the better bet. If you are saving and investing diligently, you *should* be richer later than you are today. The richer you are, the higher the percentage of your income you pay in taxes. So you need your tax break later. The Roth is also a bit more flexible in terms of getting your money out if you need to. When in doubt, go Roth.[49]

Your employer's plan: yea or nay?

Depending on your employer, the plans will be called different things but they mainly work the same. Private sector folks will be offered a 401k, government workers will be offered a Thrift Savings Plan or TSP, nonprofit peeps will be offered a 403b. Small business employees might have a SEP or a SIMPLE plan.

Your employer plan is a good start if:

- **They offer matching contributions.** (Your employer's way of bribing you to participate. You are a moron if you don't take advantage of this.)

- **It allows you to save more money than an individual plan.** Individual plans have limits as to how much money you can stuff away. Employer plans have limits, too, but they are higher.

- **Income limits prevent you from participating in an individual plan.** Sometimes you can't make an individual plan work because you make too much. Employer plans are typically free of these restrictions.

If your employer cannot offer the above, an individual retirement arrangement (IRA) is probably better for you. IRAs have more choices, and there are no hassles if you change jobs. Your "plan administrator" will be the brokerage company you open it with: Vanguard, T Rowe Price, E Trade, Fidelity, etc. The customer service crew can answer all your questions, but your most important question will be about fees.

---

49   The best argument I have heard for the *non*-Roth accounts is that when the government gives you a tax break, *take it*. If you don't take it now, they might change the rules later, in the time honored tradition of screwing the little guy. But again, invest and save wisely, and you won't be one of the little guys.

Write down *all* the fees that will be charged to you. This is the easiest way to compare. (We'll get to what to buy in Chapter 37)

You can always do something

People get freaked out about retirement accounts. They worry they are tying their money up forever. They debate Roth or non-Roth. They have no idea which brokerage firm to use. Don't worry about any of that. *Just get started.* You can always change later. You can put future allocations to a Roth, or to a non-Roth. You can switch brokerage companies. You can increase or decrease how much you contribute. So there's no excuse. Start now. And if you have already started, I say "Bravo" and ask, "Can you increase your contributions?"

Chapter 16

ESTATE PLANNING

Bored yet? If not, this chapter should do it.

Everyone needs an estate plan. If you don't have one, you've made life far more difficult for the people who survive you as they try to figure out what they are supposed to do with your money and your stuff. You might even be watching from the sidelines in the afterlife, cursing your family for dividing things up in a way far removed from your wishes.[50]

Don't talk to me about not having a big enough estate either. Money is only *part* of an estate plan. There are other parts that have nothing to do with money, parts that if ignored will make it very difficult for everyone left on planet Earth. So take your excuses elsewhere, and indulge me for a few pages.

For most individuals, an estate plan will have four basic parts: (1) *simple will,* (2) *living will,* (3) *healthcare power of attorney,* (4) a *revocable living trust.* Let's take them one by one.

When you die, you leave behind your estate. Your "estate" could be a mansion, 50 metric tons of gold bars, and the controlling stock of your railroad empire. Or your estate could be an old sock and a half-eaten bag of Doritos. Regardless of its size, your estate goes through a legal process called *probate.* This process allows your creditors (if any) to get in line and demand payment before your assets are distributed to your heirs. Should an individual or corporation - Visa, Bank of America, or Tony Soprano - believe they are entitled to some or all of your estate, they may present their case before the court.

---

50 Although there is no cursing in Heaven.

A *simple will* is a legal document that directs the courts as to how your assets are divided upon your death. It is authenticated during probate, and the court does its best to follow the wishes you outlined in your will, respecting of course any legal claims by creditors. Without such a document, the division of assets follows a government established set of rules, which are not always favorable to you depending on your state. Even when they are favorable, the process takes much longer without a will.

So wills help dead people distribute their stuff. But what about your wishes when you are alive? A *living will* is a document that provides direction as to how you want to be treated if you become incapacitated. Here's where my whole don't-give-me-that-I-don't-have-enough-money-to-justify-an-estate-plan crap comes in. Living wills have *nothing* to do with money. Failure to create such a document puts unfair pressure on family members to determine your medical treatment. What's more, without this document it can be unclear as to who actually has the final say over your health. You may want your significant other to make all healthcare decisions, but in your state that power is granted to your parents.

A *healthcare power of attorney* is a document that gives someone the authority to handle your finances (and other affairs) should you become incapacitated.[51] While a living will is concerned primarily with your health, a healthcare power of attorney is concerned with your financial affairs. Failure to have this document puts your finances into "gridlock" since the only person who can make decisions, you, is mentally unable to do so.

Finally, a *revocable living trust* provides an easy transfer of assets from you to your heirs. Contrary to popular belief, it does *not* help you shelter your money from taxes. It simply avoids probate, which can be a costly and lengthy process since it involves the court system. A revocable living trust bypasses probate, making the entire process easier and cheaper on your heirs. Another misnomer is that a revocable living trust negates the necessity for a will. You *always* need a will to direct guardianship of your children. No children? A will still covers any assets that could not be put into a revocable living trust. Typically, you don't put stuff like your

---

51   Not spring break-style incapacitated. *Permanently* incapacitated.

guitar, your clothes or your cell phone into a revocable living trust, so a will is used to direct where all that stuff goes.

A revocable living trust is not necessary for most basic estate plans. However, in recent years, their popularity has increased while their costs have declined. Often much of the costs are incurred by actually transferring assets into the trust. For instance, to put a piece of real estate into a trust it requires a new deed and, in many cases, special permission from the lender. For this reason, people opt to leave certain assets out of a trust.

More attorneys are offering "flat rate" estate planning packages to help people put together a proper estate plan. For $350-$1000, all your estate planning documents can be compiled. Estate plans usually remain static until your life situation changes (divorce, kids, more kids, another divorce) so this fee will be, for the most part, a one-time expense.

You can always do something

As I have stated many times, during the stock market crash(s) of 2008, people refused to do anything with their money. They became too scared to invest in the market (any market). While I disagreed with this strategy, I was able to convince many people to "invest" $500 in an estate plan. There is *always* something you can do, so take a few hours and get your estate squared away. Don't do it for you. Do it for the people you love.

Chapter 17

SAVING FOR COLLEGE

This chapter is easy. When it comes to saving for college, the advice is simple:

Don't.

College is expensive, and it is getting more expensive every year. More and more students are on financial aid, which means more and more students are trying to get financial aid, which means there is less financial aid to go around. So you need to do everything you can to maximize your chances at financial aid. In short, this means don't save anything in a college specific savings account and don't have anything saved in the student's name.

Financial aid is supposed to be needs based, but unfortunately it is not that simple. The trouble comes in the way that colleges calculate need. Most financial aid offices make you start by filling out a form called the FAFSA (Free Application for Federal Student Aid). Pretty much everyone has to suffer through this snore fest where both the parent and the student answer a whole bunch of questions about their financial lives.

Often, however, the process doesn't stop here. Sometimes states will have additional forms asking additional questions, and sometimes the colleges themselves will pile on more paper. All these forms are trying to reach one number, called the Expected Family Contribution or EFC.[52] This is what *you* are expected to come up with to pay for college. The federal government, the state government, and the school itself will

---

52   In my talks to parents and financial aid administrators, I refer to this as the "Oh S*** Number", since it basically telegraphs how much the college expects you to pay out of your own pocket.

(hopefully) make up the difference with grants, loans, and work study programs.

While this all sounds fair and legit, it is actually far from it. Imagine your net worth in a series of trunks, all with their lids shut. You have a trunk full of your retirement assets, another has all your precious metals, one has the value of your home, one has the cash value of your life insurance policy, and yet another has the money you have saved for college. The FAFSA form, and all of its knock off's, only look in *some* of the trunks.

The reason is simple. The EFC is supposed to determine what you can pay for college, *without ruining the rest of your financial life.* The EFC does not expect you to sell your house and live in a box so your son can go to Harvard. Nor does it ask you to liquidate your retirement account so your daughter can study music in New York City.

By putting money in certain trunks and avoiding others, you drastically increase your chances of getting more financial aid. Here's what to do:

Trunks to avoid:

- Any type of college specific investment account (such as a 529 plan)
- Any money in the child's name, as colleges will ask parents to contribute 5 cents of every dollar in "free" cash, while they will ask students to contribute 35 cents of every dollar.

Trunks that are okay:

- Making extra payments on a home loan
- Retirement accounts (either in the parent's name or the student's name)
- Cash value life insurance policies
- Gold or silver coins

A simple example:

Imagine Jon and Kate (not *that* Jon and Kate, just any Jon and Kate) just had their first child, Lucy. Having read this book, they avoid college savings. Instead, here's what they do:

First they save nothing in their child's name. They tell their parents, grandparents, aunts and uncles that if they want to buy something for Lucy's financial future, buy a silver coin.

- They take the money they save by not having a college fund and put it toward paying off their home. They also max out their retirement accounts.

- During their first meeting with a financial advisor, he pushes hard for a 529 college savings plan. He pummels them with charts about the rising costs of college and how they need to be prepared. The only thing he doesn't tell them is that he makes more money when they open a 529 and makes no money when they pay down their house quicker.

- When Lucy turns 14, she starts babysitting for neighbors. Eventually this enterprising youth forms a babysitting referral service and has three people working for her. By the time she is a sophomore in high school she has $15,000 saved up.

- The year before Lucy is about to go to college, her parents know she has too much money in her own name. The colleges will ask her to cough up 35% of that $15,000. It needs to be moved.

- Two years in a row, Lucy puts $5,000 a year into a Roth IRA. She has earned income from her business and is eligible to open a retirement account.

- She spends another $3,000 on a laptop computer.[53] She knows she is going to need it anyway, but it is better to buy it *before* she applies for financial aid.

- She spends another $2,000 on gift cards to the big box stores and airlines. Again, it's all stuff she is going to need, and it's better to make the purchase now. Gift cards can be used for anything, anytime.

- Then (finally) Lucy applies for financial aid. Only one of two things will happen:

---

53   Obviously it's an Apple.

- It works. She gets the money she needs to go where she wants to go.

- It fails. She doesn't get the money she needs to go where she wants to go. In this case, she is still okay. If necessary, she can get the $10,000 she put into the Roth out of it, without paying any taxes or penalties. (*Contributions* to a Roth can be withdrawn at any time for any reason; it is *earnings* that must remain in the account.)

- If she needs to sell the silver coins, she can. Some banks will even provide loans with the coins as collateral.

- And should she need to take on some heavy loans, her parents, who are now rather close to paying off their home, can start helping once Lucy graduates. The $200 extra dollars a month that went to the house can now be given to Lucy, as a tax-free gift, until her loans are paid off.

By using the above strategies, Lucy has maximized her chances at financial aid. Even if it doesn't work out the way she prefers, she can still get most of the money she moved.

Buuuuuuut is this ethical?

Are you "stealing" this money from people who really need it? My opinion is no, and I say this for two reasons. The first is that most Americans are not saving enough for retirement, and they are not paying their homes down fast enough. There are government loans for people who cannot afford college, but there is no such thing as a retirement loan. So even if the EFC calculation didn't work out this way, I would still recommend people save for retirement first, then pay down their home, and *then* save for college.

The second thing is that the financial aid system does need to change. Currently it punishes the savers. A parent who saves for college but sacrifices retirement savings cannot actually afford college. They may have the money, but they cannot *afford* it.

A brief word on student loans:

Student loans have become the new credit card for most Americans. Students are borrowing so much that their career choice literally cannot support the payments. Here are a few quick things to keep in mind:

- The bad news is, unlike most other loans, student loans cannot be discharged in a bankruptcy.

- The good news is, unlike most other loans, if you are having trouble with your payments, there are built in programs to help you. So don't hide. Call your lender and ask what is available.

- Students always tell me the amount they borrowed. I don't care about that. What I do care about are two things: 1) What are the monthly payments going to be after you graduate and 2) can you career choice support those payments?

- I recommend meeting with the financial aid office every semester and asking them what your monthly payments are as of today. This will give you an idea if you are borrowing too much.

- Remember college is an investment and should be treated like any other investment. In Chapter 10, I offer some great questions to ask before buying an investment. Try asking these questions about your college education.

You can always do something

Uhhhh ... actually in this chapter, you're kinda doing nothing, as in, *don't* save for your child's college education until your own investments are squared away. Also be careful with how much money you borrow for your education

---

Part 3
The Fun Stuff

WHEW! YOU MADE IT THROUGH
THE BORING STUFF. MY SINCERE HOPE
IS THAT YOU DIDN'T JUST READ IT,
YOU ACTUALLY DID IT. IF YOU DIDN'T,
BLOCK OFF TIME IN YOUR CALENDAR
RIGHT NOW TO GET THAT STUFF DONE.

Chapter 18

INVESTING VS. SAVING: THE SIMPLE DIFFERENCE EVERYONE FORGETS

Investing is the act of *risking* your resources somewhere in hopes that they will grow. Investing is different than saving. *Saving* is the act of putting your resources somewhere safe to be used later. As simple as this sounds, I am amazed at how many people screw this up.

People often will remark to me, "I am 'saving' money in my 401k account." Well, unless that money is in something super safe like a money market account; they are probably not saving; they are investing.

It may seem like a simple difference, one of those "oh-you-know-what-I-mean" kind of things. But I believe many people felt the rude awakening in 2008 because they believed their money was safe in their retirement account, and it wasn't. If it is an investment, there is *always* risk.

I also smack my head when I hear the folks who talk about no-risk investing. They argue that with enough research, planning, diversification (and most dangerous of all – algorithms) that they can eliminate nearly all risk. There are two very distinct problems with this line of thinking:

1. *It doesn't work.* Long Term Capital Management was a hedge fund founded in 1994 by John Merriweather, the former vice chairman and head of bond trading for Solomon Brothers. On the board of the fund were two economists (Myron Scholes and Robert C. Merton) who won the Nobel Prize in 1997 for a new method of determining value. In its fourth year, the fund lost $4.6 *billion*, leading to a bailout by other financial companies, supervised by

the Federal Reserve.[54] The fund depended heavily on a complex algorithm known as the Black Scholes Pricing Model. I guess the Black Scholes Pricing Model depended heavily on the Russian Financial Crisis *not* happening, which unfortunately, it did.

2. *Even when it works, it doesn't work:* I do own what I suppose these investing gurus would call a "risk-free" investment. It's a piece of property that I bought with almost no money down. I bought it with partners so the very small amount of money we did put down we shared amongst us. The property has a seller-financed, non-recourse, private mortgage, which means if I fail for any reason to make the payments, the seller simply takes the house back. No foreclosure, no dings on my credit report. Sounds risk-free, right? What these risk-free cheerleaders fail to consider is the *time* I spent finding that property. I took a *risk* spending hours and hours looking for it. Then researching it. Then negotiating to buy it. Those were hours I could have spent with my family, my friends, or at the gym.[55] My time is a resource, and I put it at risk to find this investment.

Saving

There is always a risk in investing (even if it is just your time), but with saving there should be no risk.[56] We put money into savings for only three reasons:

- **To pay for emergencies.** You already know this one, that's why you now (hopefully) have your emergency account.

- **To pay for stuff we cannot afford right now.** If you need $1,000 to buy the TV but have only $200, you'll have to either save or buy it on credit. Assuming for a moment you're not going to go the credit route, you'll need to put this money in a super safe spot. Again, this may sound simple, but I run into many people who tell me they are investing in the stock market to "save up" for a car. They've got it backwards.

---

54 This was not the first and certainly not the last of the Federal Reserve led bailouts.
55 However, we both know I would not have been at the gym. It just sounds better when I say it.
56 Well, there is always a risk. Super safe investments can be hurt by inflation, new regulations, and even catastrophic swings in the economy. But by and large our savings will not lose us more than we put in.

- **To keep some of the profits we have made.** During the dot-com boom, a friend of mine turned $250,000 into $500,000. "Ron", I said, "time to take some of those profits and put them somewhere safe." "Peter," he replied, "I just doubled my money in a few months, I am not stopping now." Several months later, Ron was up to $800,000. "Ron," said I, ""time to take some of those profits and put them somewhere safe." "Had I listened to you," he countered, "I would not be up over $500,000." A year passed, and Ron was at $1.6 million. "Ron," I began, and offered him my boilerplate spiel. "Peter, I am on a roll." He said those words in the year 2000. A year later, Ron had only $200,000 left. The crazy thing is that Ron was actually *saving* to buy a house on a lake to retire in. The lake house was going to cost $500,000. Had he taken some of his profits and kept them safe, he would have had his lake house. To this day, he does not.

Combing saving and investing

Basically all investments fall into one of two categories: *growth* investments and *income* investments. Growth investments tend to be riskier but offer a higher reward. They fluctuate more with the ups and downs of the market, so they are safest when bought with a long-term view. Income investments tend to be less risky, and therefore pay a smaller reward. They have a more predictable return.

Combining these two types of investments builds the basic investment strategy that everyone should follow. When you are young, go heavy on the growth investments and light on the income investments. Every year you age, more money should go to income and less to growth. It is important to remember that even our income investments can let us down, so we still need to save some of the profits we make from both growth and investments.

You can always do something

Saving is different from investing. Simply by knowing the difference you'll have a far more abundant financial life.

Chapter 19

INVESTING: THE BASIC IDEA AND THE BASIC PROBLEMS WITH THE BASIC IDEA

Investing, as we learned in the last chapter, is the act of risking your money in hopes that it will grow. You now know that there is always a risk, even if that risk is the consumption of your time. Unfortunately, there are other problems with investing, especially when it comes to stock market investing. I'm going to tell you what they are and what to do.

The Basic Idea

The basic idea is to invest 10% of your income (regardless of what it is) in an investment that will give you at least a 7% return. Typically this cuts out everything except stocks and real estate. If you do this for 30 years, you will have amassed a sum of money large enough, that if you can keep earning that same 7%, you will have replaced enough of your income to retire.

Here's the math on that: If you made $40,000 every year for the rest of your life, and you invested 10% of your annual income, you would invest $4,000 every year. By consistently doing this, and consistently earning 7% (after inflation) in 30 years your investments would grow to $434,000. If you kept that $434,000 in an account that kept earning 7%, you would get a paycheck of just over $30,000 a year. Since most retirement planners suggest you need at least 70% of your current income in retirement, the basic idea works. Except …

The basic problem with the Basic Idea:

Actually there is more than one.

The first problem depends entirely on:

You saving 10% of your income.

Many Americans can't even get that far. They fool themselves into thinking, "Once I get that raise, then I will invest 10%." Bull. There is always something sexier, faster, brighter, silkier, cuter, trendier, or more convenient to buy than a long-term investment. But let's assume for now you can get over the hump of saving 10%.

That brings us to the next problem:

Your income is flat for life.

The basic idea assumes you earn the same amount of money every year for the rest of your life, when in fact the opposite is true. While there are ups and downs for everyone, most people enjoy a high salary towards the end of their careers. They suffer through a low salary at the beginning.

So when you invest 10% of your income, it's the largest chunks - that 10% from the final years - that has the shortest time to grow. So you really aren't replacing your current income, you are replacing an odd mix of all your incomes.

And that brings us to the next problem:

Average returns are NOT the same as yearly returns.

This is the dirtiest secret in the world of personal finance, one that stares everyone in the face every single day, and one that every financial advisor doesn't want you to know. Here it is spelled out:

Imagine you invested $1,000 and got an "average" return of 7% per year for 5 years. Your investment chart would look something like this:

- End of Year 1: $1,070
- End of Year 2: $1,144.90
- End of Year 3: $1,225.04
- End of Year 4: $1,310.80
- End of Year 5: $1,402.55

$1,402.55 after five years. Not bad. The only problem is that stocks don't pay the same return every year. They fluctuate drastically. Let's look at what happens when the *average* return remains 7%, but the *yearly* returns fluctuate:

- In year one you have a $1,000 investment and the stock market goes *down* 10%. At the end of year one you have $900.

- In year two, the market goes up 15% so at the end of the year you have $1,035.

- In year three, the market goes up again, but only by 4%. Now your account holds $1,076.40.

- Year four is an incredible year with a whopping 35% return. Your account soars to $1,453.14.

- However, year five sees a bit of a drop, losing 9%. You now have $1,322.36.

In both cases, you have an *average* return of 7%. However, in the second case you ended up with $80 less. I admit, $80 is not a ton of money, but ask anyone who planned on retiring in 2008 when the market plummeted, just how happy they were relying on the "average investment return" charts.

So now that the secret is out, what do you do about it? "Hindsight wisdom is of no use," goes the old Indian proverb. Sure in 2009, any idiot can look at a stock chart and claim, "Ya shoulda sold in 2007!" But where was that idiot in 2007?

No one, and I do repeat *no one,* knows exactly when to buy or sell. Occasionally someone gets it exactly right, and when they do their typical next step is to put this prediction into a newsletter and try to get you to subscribe to it. But doing this consistently, especially with the market as a whole, is extremely difficult.

There are two techniques that, while unable to predict the exact tops and bottoms, do aid considerably in avoiding the pitfalls and grabbing the bargains. Those two strategies are known as *rebalancing* and *dollar cost averaging.*

Dollar Cost Averaging

Dollar cost averaging is the practice of investing the same amount of money at predetermined intervals into the stock market. You may, for instance, decide to invest $200 per month into the stock market. If the stock market soars to new heights, you invest the $200. If it crashes, you still invest the $200. By investing the same amount, you ensure that you buy fewer shares when prices are high and more shares when prices are low. For instance:

- In Month 1, Google is selling for $10 a share (I wish) so you would buy 20 shares.

- In Month 2, Google jumps to $50 a share, so you grab only 4 shares.

Even though Google is going up and down, you are not trying to guess the highs and lows. Indeed, it would be great if you could have bought all your shares in Month One, and then sold them in Month Two. But to do this consistently is very difficult.[57]

Dollar cost averaging takes the emotion out of it, and that is the whole key. By relying on numbers - $200 a month, every month - and not emotion, you're more likely to come out ahead over the long term.

Rebalancing

Rebalancing is a technique that would have helped many people in the stock market crash, err...*crashes* of 2008. There are a few different ways to do this, but my favorite involves taking your age and subtracting it from 100. The answer is the percentage of your portfolio that should be in the risky stuff. The remaining amount should be in super safe investments.

A 50-year-old woman, for example, would subtract her age from 100 and put 50% of her money in super safe havens - cash, CDs, government bonds, and paying down debt - and the remainder of the money should be in stuff that will (hopefully) get some growth - real estate, stocks and precious metals. Every quarter she "rebalances" her portfolio, to keep that 50/50 split. When she turns 51, she rebalances again with 49% in the risky stuff and 51% in the safe stuff.

---

57 Although, in an upcoming Chapter, we'll talk a strategy that just might work.

Here's how this helps protect you. Imagine in 2007 that she had $50,000 in safe stuff and $100,000 in the risky stuff. The growth investments have done well due to the bull market of the previous few years.[58] But, based on her age, she needs to rebalance. She sells $25,000 worth of stock and puts it somewhere safe. Her balance is now $75,000 safe, $75,000 growth.

Then along comes 2008. The market drops considerably and her new portfolio is $75,000 in safe investments and a sad $32,000 in growth products. Her portfolio again is out of whack, only this time in the other direction. Bravely, she moves $21,500 out of the safe stuff and puts it into the riskier investments. The market does go back up, and there is much rejoicing, but perhaps none louder than hers, for she had the courage to sink money in when times looked the toughest.

Rebalancing is not perfect, but it can help you take some profits during the market highs and grab the bargains at the market lows. How often you should do it is really up to you. I think once every quarter is enough, plus anytime you hear drastic news about the stock market. The news could be drastically good or drastically bad; it doesn't really matter. If it is drastic, then it is worth looking at your portfolio to consider making some readjustments.

The one thing, or two things rather, to watch out for when rebalancing, are taxes and fees. In a tax-favored, discount brokerage stock account, rebalancing is easy. Fees are almost nil, and taxes are delayed or gone completely. You can move money back and forth with little hassle on you and your wallet. Outside of these accounts, or with a full-service stock broker, you need to be more careful.

Rebalancing also creates some problems when we look at investments other than stocks. The commissions on gold and silver can be pretty steep or if you invest in real estate by buying rental properties you can't sell 10% of a property. It's all or nothing. And if one of your "investments" is paying down debt, once you've used it, you cannot get it back.

The way around all this is to simply allocate future funds towards something else. If you were investing $100 a month in silver and silver

---

58 When the market is headed up, it's called a bull market. Bulls are animals that charge. When the market is headed down, it's called a bear market. Bears are animals that sleep (hibernate) for long periods of time..

climbs to a point where it puts your portfolio out of whack, consider easing up on future investments rather than selling the silver outright.

Rebalancing is easy, and it would have saved a lot of folks over the last ten years, when the stock market looked like this:

No one can predict exactly when the ups and downs you see above will occur. With enough research, people can at times get close. But I prefer the simpler system of rebalancing.

Our sample 50-year-old woman should also use dollar cost averaging to align with her portfolio. If she was investing say $600 a month, she would put $300 of that $600 into her supersafe investments (because she is 50 and that's 50% of her future contributions) and the other $300 into the growth stuff.

You can always do something

People got very frustrated in 2008, relying on the much adored charts that assumed an average return of 7% per year. It doesn't work out that way. But it's not so horrible that you need to hide from the investment world forever. You still need to invest 10% of your income for retirement. Dollar cost averaging and rebalancing can help you flatten out those crazy market swings.

Chapter 20

HOW TO EVALUATE AN INVESTMENT

Your Uncle Lou comes to you and offers you a 25% slice of his new pizza parlor. He just needs $50,000. Is it worth it? Gold is currently around $1,600 an ounce. Should you buy? You are considering starting your own business, an ironic travel agency that specializes in travel agents, and you'll need about $10,000 to start it. Is that smart?

Trying to determine if an investment is a good deal is not easy. But by asking the following questions, you can get a lot closer a lot quicker to figuring out if a particular play is right for you.

Ten important questions:

When considering an investment or when one is being "pushed" on you, ask yourself:

1. **What would I buy if I did not buy this?** The economists refer to this as "opportunity cost." Money put "here" cannot also be put "there."

2. **Assuming I do decide to buy, where else could I buy it?** Is there a cheaper place? A place that doesn't charge a commission? Lower fees? A way to buy it without paying taxes – like in a Roth IRA?

3. **Do I understand what this investment is and how it works?** I am shocked by how many people get this wrong. Think about it. How many people do you know who own a fancy-sounding stock like Solar Crystal Armored Munitions, a.k.a. SCAM, without knowing what exactly the company does?

4. **How do I get paid from this investment?** Is it all at once? Monthly? Through growth? Through income? Knowing *when* you will get your money is almost as important as how much you will get.

5. **How does this investment fit into my goals and overall financial plan?** Remember an investment can be more valuable to you than to your neighbor. If you have no investments in precious metals, a precious metals investment might be more valuable to you than your neighbor because you need it for diversification.

6. **How do this compare to the risk free rate of return?** The risk free rate of return is the rate you can earn putting your money in something super safe, like a bank CD or a US government bond. The investment you are considering better beat this rate, if not, just stick with the safe stuff.

7. **Before I buy this, have I done all the simple stuff first?** For example, have you paid off credit card debt, secured the proper insurance etc.?

8. **What are the potential problems with this investment?** What are the fees associated with it? What could go wrong? What is the worst thing that could happen?[59]

9. **Is this investment heavily dependent on another industry to be successful?** For example a defense company might be heavily dependent on which political party is in office, while an automaker is heavily dependent on a strong economy. A food manufacturer is not.

10. **What are the tax consequences of buying (or selling) this investment?** Ask your tax advisor on this one.

By simply running through these questions in your head, you can protect yourself from a sleazy salesperson and perhaps from the most dangerous person of all: *you.* More often than not, it isn't an outsider who screws up our financial life, it's us. We get emotional, either out of fear or greed, and we do something stupid. We jump in too late or we jump out too soon. These questions will force you to take a few deep breaths, calm down and think – three things people spend very little time doing when it comes to their financial lives.

---

59   Besides the Mayan Calendar actually coming true.

You can always do something

And in this case "something" is slowing down. Most people invest based on fear and greed, and both are dangerous. Hastily running into real estate is just as dangerous as hastily running away from it. Calm yourself down by asking these questions.

Chapter 21

THE STOCK MARKET

I am always surprised by the surprising number of people invested in the stock market, be it through some sort of retirement plan or otherwise, who surprisingly have no idea how it actually works. So before we get to what to buy, let's take a look at how a stock becomes a stock that is listed on a market.

A stock is a share of a company. Stockholders are owners in a company. *Every* company has at least one stockholder. If you own your own landscaping business, and it's just you, a mower, two rakes and a shovel, you are the sole stockholder. Granted, you are not like Coca-Cola, which has millions of stockholders all over the world. But really there is only one difference between your company and theirs, aside from their size. That difference is your company is private, and Coca Cola, which began (as all companies do) as a private company, is now *public*. Companies make the leap from private to public for only one reason: They need money.

Businesses need money to expand, and there are only two ways to get it: Borrow it or give up a piece of the action. New companies often have trouble borrowing money, especially a lot of money, because they are not established. Banks, as Bob Hope once joked, will lend you the money as soon as you can prove you don't need it. Most companies need to go with option two, selling a piece of the pie.

Lenders expect to be paid back their money, with a predetermined interest rate, within a predetermined period of time. That's a lot of restrictions for a new company. So instead, the new company sells shares, and investors hand over their money. In this option, there are no such restrictions. If the company does well and makes money, the shareholders get paid.

If it doesn't, they won't.

When companies are seeking investors, they can do it one of two ways. They can do it privately – asking family, friends, and fools – or they can do it publicly, by asking *everyone*. If a business needs to raise a lot of money, like several hundred million dollars, family and friends usually don't cut it. So they go the public route by enlisting the help of an investment bank, which will conduct an *Initial Public Offering or IPO*. This event is the first time shares in a private company are available to the public. People who buy shares are now owners.

Yes, yes, yes. But then what? Where do these people sell their shares if they want to dump them? That is where the stock market comes in. The stock market provides a place where people can trade their stocks. After an IPO, a company becomes listed on a *stock exchange*, be it the New York Stock Exchange, the American Stock Exchange, or an overseas stock exchange. Here, all the stocks, on that particular exchange, are traded every day.

Prices of stocks are set by only one thing, the number of buyers and sellers. More people buying will drive a stock price up. A lot of sellers will cause a price to plummet. People buy out of greed and sell out of fear, and it's important to recognize this may *or may not* have anything to do with the actual performance of the company.

For years, Amazon.com was losing money, yet people still bought it and the stock price went up. On the other end, H&R Block held a near monopoly in its industry for what seemed like forever, but because investors never really got excited about it, its stock price remained flat for quite some time.

Investors can make money by buying a stock at one price and selling it at higher price. They can also make money by borrowing a stock from someone else, *selling* it at a high price and then buying it back when it goes down. They then return the lower priced stock they just bought to the owner they borrowed it from. This is known as short selling or *shorting* the market. It is one of the few investments that carries *unlimited* risk, so we won't talk much about it here. But one can make money whether the stock market goes up or down.

There is a third way to make money, and that is through *dividends*. Companies are here to make a profit, and if things are going really well, they can send some of these profits to the shareholders by paying a dividend. Typically bigger, older established companies pay dividends. The smaller companies reinvest their profits right back into the business.

Stock market activity is referred to as *volume*. A lot of trading (either a lot of buying, a lot of selling, or a lot of both) would constitute heavy volume. The nightly news cares a lot about volume, but I don't, and you shouldn't either.

What you should care about are the indexes. Currently there are thousands of stocks available in the United States alone. It's too cumbersome to look at every single stock individually to see where the economy is at and to guess where it's headed. So indexes were created, the most famous being the Dow Jones Industrial Average. This horrifically unrepresentative index (made up of only 30 companies) commands unwavering loyalty from the financial world, as it is quoted daily in the global media. But apparently when this goes up, the market as a whole is doing well and when it goes down, the market as a whole is also down.

Two comprehensive indexes I like:

- **The Morgan Stanley EAFE index:** This consists of companies in Europe, Australia and the Far East.

- **The Wilshire 5000 Index:** This is a far more comprehensive index than the Dow Jones, consisting of more than 5,000 companies in the United States.

I am not a big fan of getting too worried about the daily ups and downs of the indexes. I do ask people to pay attention when the news gets really good or really bad, because it may be a good time to rebalance your portfolio. So keep a casual eye on the indexes.

So that's how the stock market works. The question now is what do you buy? Turn the page to find out.

You can always do something

These last few chapters may feel short on action items. But understanding how things work is an important action item in itself.

Chapter 22

WHAT TO BUY

Stock market investors come in only one of two boxes: Those who believe they can beat the market averages, and those who cannot.

The latter group believes in something called the *random walk* theory. In short, that theory claims that everything that can be known about a stock is already reflected in its current price. Therefore, no amount of research will provide you with an advantage. These individuals suggest buying investments that mirror the market averages. (Those indexes we discussed in the previous chapter.) We'll talk about those in a minute.

Those who believe they can beat it argue it is not a stock market but a market of stocks. You can beat the market with enough research, and they point to the people who have consistently beaten it (Warren Buffet, Peter Lynch, George Soros, and Jim Kramer before the TV show).

I take a simpler view: I have a life to live. So I am either going to accept the market average returns or pick stocks using a very simple formula.[60] In this chapter we'll talk about how to at least achieve the market averages. In a later chapter - I won't tell you which because I want you to keep reading - I will reveal a formula that has a history of beating the market, a history that is likely to continue, even if we all start doing it. But more on that later. For now we need to talk about mutual funds.

Mutual funds

Mutual funds were created many moons ago to help more people get involved in the stock market, especially the people who A) couldn't afford to otherwise and B) wanted to take the hands-off approach. A *mutual*

---

60   And by "simple" it must be so simple that even I can understand it.

fund is a money pool made up of thousands of investors just like you and me. We invest our money into the fund, and in doing so surrender control over to a professional manager.

The manager now has a substantial amount of money to invest ($100 million on the small end and several billion on the large end) because thousands of us pooled our money together. A full-time staff assists the manager in finding the best stocks for our fund. We don't own the stocks, the fund owns the stocks, and we own shares in the fund. Every day the value of the fund is calculated by adding up the prices of all the investments held in the fund and dividing the number of outstanding shares to determine the price per share. This value is called the *net asset value* (NAV). The manager charges a management fee to pick these stocks for us, usually somewhere between 1% and 3% per year of NAV.[61]

There are two types of mutual funds: *managed* and *unmanaged*. A managed fund is the one described above. Basically there is a dude or a dudette buying and selling the stocks in the fund. An unmanaged fund has no dude, rather the stocks are bought and sold using a computer program. Unmanaged funds don't "select" stocks, they simply buy everything in the particular market index they are tracking. So an unmanaged Wilshire 5000 Index Fund will buy every stock in the Wilshire 5000 Index. Unmanaged funds are often called *index funds* for this reason.

The main advantage of unmanaged funds is that the expenses are lower. A fund with a 2% management fee is already 1% behind a fund with only a 1% fee. Index funds usually have management fees *below* 0.5%, giving them a huge advantage right out of the gate.

There are other problems with managed funds, a main one being higher turnover. *Turnover* refers to the amount a mutual fund buys and sells. A $100 million fund that bought and sold $80 million worth of stock in one year has an 80% turnover rate. High turnover rates mean the manager is often forced to sell stocks he doesn't want to sell, simply because shareholders in the fund want their cash. Lots of turnover also means the fund is paying commissions on those purchases and sales (because yes, mutual funds do pay commissions). And turnover aside,

---

61   Some mutual funds carry another fee called a *load*, which is a commission charged when it is bought or sold. I recommend buying only no-load funds. Remember, commissions cut right into profits.

the most frustrating aspect of managed funds is even if you do find a star manager, after five or ten years of stellar performance, they retire.

ETFs

I think most people are better off going with index mutual funds. In fact, there is a very specific type of index fund I like: an *exchange traded fund or ETF*. Remember how regular funds calculate their daily value or NAV? Regular funds are not listed on an exchange, so the price has to be calculated this way. Shares of an ETF, as the name states, are listed on an exchange. The price fluctuates based on the number of buyers and sellers, just like a stock.

ETFs that follow an index are typically a better bet over regular index funds because:

- Generally, they have lower expenses (even lower than regular index funds).
- Tax-wise, you come out better (usually).
- 'Tis a bit easier to get your money out if you need it.

'Okay Pete', you say as you read this, 'enough talking. WTF do I buy?' Basically you'll want to diversify, putting as much into tax-advantaged accounts as possible:

- On the growth side:
    - Funds that track a U.S. company index (such as the Wilshire 5000)
    - Funds that track foreign companies (such as the Morgan Stanley EAFE Index)
    - Funds that track REITs (A great fund is the Vanguard REIT Index)[62]
    - Maybe a precious metals index fund (But consider owning at least some physical metals. I discuss a rather cool way to do this in Chapter 29)
    - Possibly a rental property (We'll get to this more in Chapter 25)

---

62 REITs don't buy stocks, instead they buy huge pieces of real estate like shopping malls, sports stadiums, and skyscrapers. You and I can't afford to buy these properties on our own, so we buy them through REITs.

- On the safe and income side:

    - You'll also need a super safe cash fund that you sweep profits into or pull from when prices plunge. Every IRA and employer's plan has one of these. Ask them for suggestions.

    - A cash value life insurance policy: Not for everyone, but we'll discuss this more in Chapter 30.

    - Income funds: As you get older, more and more of your money will be in income funds. These are funds that invest in safer stocks, large established companies that pay dividends. They may not be index funds so just watch the expense fees.

    - Individual bonds: Your employer's plan will have a bond fund. Whatever it is, I will not be a fan. But individual bonds have their place, especially for folks closer to their golden years. The next chapter can help.

You can always do something

If your company offers a retirement plan, call or visit the plan administrator. (Sometimes, for big companies that person comes to your office.) Tell them you are looking for the ETFs or index funds that meet the above. Ask about all fees. The plan administrator might not be able to create this exact mix but she'll get close enough. What she cannot accommodate in your employer's plan, any of the major brokerage companies, such as Vanguard, Fidelity, T. Rowe Price, etc., can help with in an individual retirement arrangement. Don't focus too much on past performance – stick to index funds and even better, index ETFs as much as possible. And watch those fees.

Chapter 23

BONDS

Meh.

Bonds are IOUs. They are loans issued by corporations and governments. If one of these two entities needs money, they can try to get a loan from a bank, but they may have a cheaper and easier time by issuing bonds

Imagine that Microsoft needs $10 million.[63] They might issue 10,000 5-year, $1,000 bonds with a 5% coupon. If you purchased one of these puppies, you would hand $1,000 to Microsoft, and then Microsoft would hand you a piece of paper worth $1,000 in 5 years. But that piece of paper also entitles you to receive 5% of the face value of that bond every year (a.k.a. the "coupon"), in this case $50. So bonds can be a boring way to build wealth.

But here is where they get interesting. Bonds trade in the open market and their market price varies based on interest rates. Suppose you bought the above bond, and then interest rates dropped to around 2%. Your bond is paying 5%, but every other bozo can only get 2%. So your bond is now worth more than its $1,000 face value. You could sell it at a higher price.

Of course, this can go the other way. If interest rates shoot up to 7%, well, now who is the bozo? Your bond is not worth as much. Bonds have a safety net, in that if you hold them until they mature, you will get all the money originally agreed to. This is why financial educators don't get too excited about bond mutual funds, because often the manager is forced to sell the bonds before maturity, forfeiting their built in safety net.

---

63 They don't, but go with me.

I think the best "bond" out there is to aggressively pay down debt. Paying down debt is tax free, because you are not earning any income. It's also risk free. You can't lose any money because you are already losing it! And remember, not losing money is the same as earning it.

> ## Not losing money is the same as earning it.

If you do want to dabble in bonds, I think bonds issued by the U.S. Treasury are a good place start. The two I like are I Bonds, and 5-Year Treasury Notes. Because interest rates are ridiculously low, these bonds aren't paying much in interest, so don't get too excited. Then again, neither are anyone else's bonds. Bonds issued by the U.S. Government are super safe, and you can sell them at any time, although selling some bonds early will force you forfeit some interest.[64]

We'll talk about this more in Chapter 36, but many smart people believe we are headed either for serious *deflation* or serious *inflation*. If we get deflation, then interest rates will go down. Longer term U.S. Treasuries will be the best protection here. If, on the other hand, we get inflation, then interest rates will rise, and I Bonds, which protect against inflation, will be the best bet.

Since I can't be for sure who is right, I am suggesting you buy a little of both. I Bonds can be bought for as little as $25, Treasuries for

---

64 The U.S. Government can of course default on its debt, and it recently suffered the first credit rating downgrade in history. Should a default occur, that would be very ugly (just ask the Russians) and that is why in Chapter 29 we'll talk about investing in silver.

as little as $100. So you are not making any giant commitments here. Even though we are *planning* to hold these bonds at least five years, you can dump them anytime you want. You won't get rich (especially with today's interest rates), but they can be a good place to park your cash after a rebalance.

You can always do something

Interest rates are very low as I write this, so bonds are probably not the best place to be, but a tiny portfolio of U.S. government bonds can hardly hurt for someone still too scared of the stock market and precious metals markets. Take ten minutes and set up an account at www.treasurydirect.gov, which is the government's website for buying these bonds. (This site even has educational videos!) Since you can buy all these bonds in very tiny amounts, you're not betting the farm on any one purchase. But remember the best bond of all is stepping up payments on an adjustable rate loan. Start there first. Also ask your retirement account administrator - be it IRA or employer - how you go about buying government bonds inside your retirement account. Oh, and uhhh, if you care for a bit more reward, and inevitably, more risk, visit the Resources section of my website www.peterbielagus.com and read the ebook on "Becoming a Private Lender."

Chapter 24

HOME SAVING

There are several reasons why we are in the current mortgage crisis.

Indeed, there were more than a few pushy mortgage brokers and real estate agents guilty of putting someone in a house or loan they could not afford. There were slightly fewer who actually broke the law in doing so. However, much of this disaster could have been avoided had more homebuyers followed the immutable laws of home buying. Show me someone who followed _all_ these commandments and _still_ suffered foreclosure, and I will show you a rare person indeed. Those laws are:

- **Do not buy a home with an adjustable rate mortgage.**
- **Put _at least_ 10 percent down.**
- **The size of the loan cannot be more than 3 times your annual income.**
- **Plan on staying in the home _at least_ five years.**
- **Plan on putting 5% of the mortgage payment into a savings fund for home repairs.**

Feel free, of course, to break any and all of these rules (On my first home purchase, I broke them all.). Millions of Americans did the same and have managed to keep their homes. But when someone decides to break these rules, they drastically increase their chances of a foreclosure. Granted, their house might be worth less than they bought it, but by following these rules they would still be able to afford it without destroying their finances. Let's dissect each rule to find out why:

- **Do not buy a home with an adjustable rate mortgage**. Predictability is of immeasurable value in the world of personal finance. Knowing how much money you will need next month is as precious as the money itself. An adjustable rate mortgage prevents you from knowing this. Believe it or not, even people with *fixed* rate mortgages are subject to increases at any time, because their taxes and insurance premiums can go up. Often municipalities (for reasons I still cannot figure out) will double, even triple, their tax rates in one year, rather than institute slight increases over time. It's a political thing, I suppose, but to the savvy budgeter, it's Armageddon. Home ownership has enough unpredictability fnot to mention leaky roofs to tax hikes, from insurance increases to overall market fluctuations. Don't add anymore with an adjustable rate.

> Knowing how much money you will need next month is as precious as the money itself.

- **Put at least 10% down**. People often ask me what the big deal about 10% is. "Aside from protecting the bank," they argue, "what's the big deal as long as my salary can handle the payments?" Indeed, the biggest benefactor of you putting 10% down isn't you, it is the bank. But the 10% goal does have an often unmentioned benefit to you. It teaches you how to save. Gathering up a 10% down payment, regardless of the home's price, is no easy task. It takes discipline, a discipline that may come in handy should the real estate market not go your way.

- **The size of the loan cannot be more than 3 times your annual income.** In most markets, the lender takes care of this for you. With a few exceptions, they won't let you borrow any more then three times your annual income to buy a home. However, the rules began to loosen in the late 1990's and people began borrowing more than 10 *times* their annual income. (Some borrowers had no income at all!) The regulations have once again been tightened.

- **Plan on staying in the home at least five years.** Five seems to be a magic number in real estate. Markets go up and down, and they can stay down for a while, but five years will protect you from getting clobbered by those ups and downs. While the real estate market can go up and down just like the stock market, a real estate investment has the advantage of debt pay down. With every month that passes, the debt on the property gets a little bit smaller. Every year, more of your payments go towards the principal of the loan as opposed to the interest. So not only does five years protect you from the market swings, it also allows those principal payments to build up a large enough cushion.[65]

- **Plan on putting 5% of the mortgage payment into a savings fund for home repairs.** Even if you were lucky enough to have your home skyrocket in value, you can't get that cash until you sell it. During that time, the home will cost you money in terms of mortgage payments, taxes and repairs. Your bank will remind you to pay the loan. The government will remind you to pay the taxes. But you need to put some money away for repairs and 5% of the monthly mortgage payment is a good rule of thumb.

If you can stick to these rules, you will steer clear of a lot of trouble in the housing world.

Buuuut ummmm...

What do I do if I am about to lose my house? Or already lost it? Then what?

---

65   And yes, I realize people purchased homes that will take longer to recover. Remember, if it is an investment, there is *always* a risk. But for the *nation*, the five-year rule would have prevented a lot of the reckless "flipping" of houses ... a very lucrative venture until the music stops.

Already Gone

If you already lost your house, there are two things you need to know. The first is that your credit score took a hit if there was a foreclosure. Consult Chapter 14 for help on rebuilding that. The second thing is that if you "voluntarily" lost your home by selling it for *less* than what you owed (a.k.a a *short sale*), then the bank has two options about the additional money owed:

1. **They can ask you to make up the shortfall.** So if you owed $200,000 and the bank sold the house for $180,000 after all commissions, you will owe the bank $20,000. That is unless …

2. **You can get them to forgive all or part of that debt.** Keep in mind, however, that forgiven debt could be taxable as income, so you may have to report it as if you *earned* that $20,000.00. Rules on this are constantly changing, so be sure to ask your tax advisor.

When is it time to walk?

If you are still hanging on, it may, unfortunately, make sense to walk away. This isn't so much about the price of the house; rather it's about your ability to make the payments. A house that is worth $30,000 less than its loan is far from worthless. But if hanging onto the house will deplete your other savings and investments, it may be time to go. If a rising interest rate, insurance premiums, or just too much darn house are going to wipe you out, it's better to leave sooner rather than later.

Hanging in there

Okay, I hate to preen too much, but unless you got flat out swindled (and many Americans did), you did sign an agreement to pay back the loan. So finances aside, you should try to make every effort to pay it back, even if it creates a temporary inconvenience in your life. You may, for instance, have to take in a roommate or get off your butt and finally build that deck out back to increase the resale value of your home.

Be sure to consider *all* the costs of owning that home, both bad *and good*. For instance, if you move, you'll have to pay moving expenses. Don't forget, you can deduct the interest on the loan payments, and every payment you make pays off a wee bit of principal. Remember Old Gil from Chapter 1? He lost $100 a month for 30 years and he still made out okay. Don't run from your house just because everyone else has.

Negotiating with Your Bank

This is either going to be easy or hard, and unfortunately for most folks it is going to be hard. The reason why is there are only two types of home loans – *portfolio loans* and *non-portfolio loans*. If yours is a portfolio loan, you're lucky. If not, ya got some fightin' to do.

When a bank "portfolios" a loan, that simply means it doesn't sell it to someone else. Usually smaller banks and credit unions do this with their home loans. Banks also do it with the nonstandard loans, like commercial mortgage loans and business lines of credit. Because the bank owns the loan, you can talk directly with the bank.

If this is you, then do so. Write out a plan of what you want from them and how this will ensure they will get paid. Approach them for a meeting, and if they refuse, send them a letter stating you were disappointed they would not meet. A bank refusing to work with you will lose a lot of credibility if they ever have to take you to court.

Keep at it. You can always do something! Want some inspiration? Read this:

TRUE STORY

A friend of mine was underwater with her home. She did, however, have a plan to pay back the bank; she just needed a little help. She called and called customer service, waited on hold forever, could recite the background music verse for verse and never got anywhere. Eventually, she gave up calling.

Instead, she found the regional headquarters of the bank, and drove 2 hours to meet with a senior vice president. She, of course, did not have a meeting with the senior vice president, so she waited in the lobby for him. *For six hours.* The receptionist politely tried to shoo her away, but my friend wouldn't budge. She just sat in the lobby with her book and, in a modern display of civil disobedience, wouldn't budge until the senior vice president emerged.

Believe it or not, he did, and they worked something out.

Non portfolio loans

A nonportfolio loan is a loan that gets sold to the secondary market. Investors buy loans from banks to collect the interest payments, and banks sell their loans to free up cash to make new loans. The biggest buyer of home loans in the United States are the currently scandal-laden, quasi-government agencies of Fannie Mae and Freddie Mac.[66]

These agencies were designed to buy home loans so banks could free up cash to help new prospective homebuyers. Fannie and Freddie basically buy a bunch of loans, put them together in a bundle, and then slice up that bundle into something called a *tranche.* Bonds are then formed around the tranches, and investors buy those bonds. So everyday investors, like your mom, your uncle, and most of Iceland, bought these bonds that were backed by American home loans.

Well, you know what happened. Many of those home loans were made to unqualified borrowers, and many borrowers were flat out lied to. Which means investors didn't get their payments on time, so lenders had to foreclose on houses that were suddenly worth much less than the loans they were wrapped in.

This means, to you as a homeowner, that your loan isn't a loan anymore. It was shredded up into tranches, and the tranches were turned into bonds. Your bills are sent to a servicing company, but they don't own the loan, so they can't technically agree to reduce your interest rate.[67]

Okay, after rereading the history of the mortgage crisis, a story you have no doubt read before, there is some good news. The banks, even the

---

66 Fannie Mae is the nickname for the Federal National Mortgage Association and Freddie Mac is the nickname for Federal Home Loan Mortgage Association.
67 Here is another dirty little secret in the mortgage world. Between you and the bank is a servicing company that collects the payments. If you begin to pay late, the servicing company gets to charge you late fees. Often the servicer makes *more* money when you pay late, because they can charge these fees. If you stop paying altogether, they will eventually foreclose. But the servicing company gets paid *first*, before your bank. Often banks want to work something out, but servicing companies do not.

ones that sell their loans, are starting to help. And after passing a series of absolutely wonderful refinance programs that no one qualified for, the government is finally starting to get it. So don't hide. Call them.

You can always do something

If you are a new homebuyer, stick to the immutable laws of home buying as best you can. If, on the other hand, you are in trouble, don't hide. Check your bank's website. Check my website www. peterbielagus.com under the Resource's section. Then call your bank. There will be a special 800 number to call if you expect to have trouble paying your mortgage. Plan on being on hold for a week and take good notes of what you talk about. It won't be easy, but the worst thing you can do is nothing.

Chapter 25

REAL ESTATE

The last chapter was more about how to save a house, rather than how to buy one. While millions of Americans are in a bind with their current home, there are also millions of renters who are looking at a rare buying opportunity. As I write this, both prices *and* interest rates are low, a mix we don't see often. So here are some tips to snag either your dream home or an investment property.

Buying real estate

- **Grab the grants.** Federal, state and even local governments offer programs to help you buy a home. Most of these grants cannot be used to buy investment properties, only your primary residence. Tighter still, you often need to be a first-time homebuyer in that state.[68] But grant money is about as free as you can get, so you might as well grab it. Just be aware of the restrictions associated with the grants. A common one, for instance, is that you must live in the house for a certain number of years. If you sell it before that, you'll have to pay back some or all of the grant.

- **Know that lenders and real estate agents sometimes hate grants.** There is more paperwork for them, and it can take longer for them to get paid. So just take their advice with a grain of salt, if they are encouraging you to avoid the grants. Typically they are a good deal.

---

68   The good news is that you may not need to be a "true" first timer. Sometimes states define a first-time homebuyer as someone who hasn't bought a home in the last five years. Be sure to investigate.

- **The most important number no one shows you.** That number is the DOM or Days On Market. Real estate agents can see it in their property search functions, but in the ones they send to you, that number is suspiciously left out. Be sure to ask for it. If a property has been on the market for a long time, it's a good candidate for a bargain.

- **Know who is in bed with who.** Most real estate transactions start with a buyer finding a real estate agent. The real estate agent will help you find a mortgage broker, a title company, an attorney, and a home inspector. Just remember that *all* these people get referrals from the real estate agent. While they cannot pay her a direct commission for referring you, they can sponsor an open house for her or contribute to her marketing expenses. You may buy one house every five years. But she will refer a buyer to this group once a week. You tell me, where does the loyalty lie? Just be aware of who really represents who. Feel free to find your own home inspector, your own lender, and your own title company.

- **Know that real estate agents don't want top dollar, they want a quick sale.** This dirty little secret was exposed in the book *Freakonomics*, but real estate agents - and I am one - have known it forever. A typical commission on a home sale, is about 4%-6% of the sales price. So a 5% commission on a $200,000 home yields a $10,000 commission. That $10,000 is typically split between the seller's agent and the buyer's agent. But when the seller's agent walks away with her $5,000, she has to split half of that with her office, so on a $200,000 sale she winds up with only $2,500.

Now $2,500 is not chump change. But what *is* chump change is the extra money she would have gotten if the house sold for $210,000. That $10,000 extra dollars is worth a lot to you as the seller, but it's only $125 more to the agent. If, in that time of holding out for a higher offer, she had to host three more open houses and drive to the property to show it five more times, that extra $125 really isn't worth her effort. She, like all real estate agents, wants a quick sale.[69]

---

69   This is not to pummel agents too hard. Often sellers hold out for the highest offer, only to discover too late that last offer was in fact the highest offer. Buyers, too, sometimes get so focused on the price, they forget the cost of their time, schlepping from open house to open house every Sunday trying to find a bargain.

- **You make your profit when you *buy* not when you sell.** Of course you hand over money when you buy and (hopefully) get money when you sell. However, we get our profits by locking in a great house at a good price. So spend a good deal of time looking and making a lot of offers. It costs nothing but your time to make an offer. If it takes you an extra 100 hours to save $10,000 off the price, you just got paid $100 an hour to make those aggressive offers.

- **Can't afford to buy it? Consider *optioning* it.** While I am not a fan of optioning stocks, optioning real estate is a whole different ball game. The reason is because you have so much more control. Suppose in your town every house sits on a one-acre lot. Two acres is very rare and therefore very valuable. You see a house that is on 1.1 acres. But what is interesting is there is a vacant lot right next to the house that is only 0.9 acres. Put them together, and you would have a two acre lot. But you wouldn't want to buy one until you are sure you could buy the other. So you option them both. You buy the *right* to buy them at a later date for a predetermined price. Once you have control of both, you buy both. So where can you get a copy of a standard option agreement? Just visit my website www.peterbielagus.com and look under the Resources section.

- **Consider seller financing.** Banks are a bit tight fisted these days. They don't want to lend money to anyone that falls short of absolutely perfect. If your situation isn't such (and no one's is) you might want to look around for a property with seller financing. Instead of borrowing the money from the bank, you borrow it from the seller. For this to work, the seller needs to have little or no debt on their house. If that's the case, rather than receiving one lump payment from you at closing, they instead agree to receive the payments for a period of x years. Since the seller has no debt on their house, they don't need a big check to pay off a bank. They can accept the money over time.

- **Hire a home inspector.** These guys walk through the house and look for what's wrong with it. While they can't see through walls, they occasionally find something big. (My guy saved me $2,000 in his inspection. Thanks home inspector guy.)[70]

---

70   I can't remember his name. F something. Frank? Fred?

- **Shop the financing.** Real estate gets its value from two places: the location of the structure itself and the financing wrapped around it. A property can become more valuable through better financing just as it can through a new coat of paint. Ask your loan officer to discuss the *yield spread premium.* This sneaky number was hidden from consumers during the mortgage boom. However, new regulations require it to be spelled out on loan documents. Still, many people don't know what it is. It basically compares the "cost" of the loan to the lender against what you pay. Your lender might be able to "borrow" $100,000 at 5%, and he loans it to you at 5.5%, making the yield spread 0.5%. Simply by asking this question, you'll appear smarter than he originally thought, and it will keep him on his toes.

You can always do something

Many people are not in a position to buy a home or investment property. If you are one of the few, it's worth it to start looking around. The real estate market may go even lower, but in every community there are properties that do well regardless of the economy. Take the time to find those gems. Most economists agree rents will be going up, whether we have inflation or deflation. It costs nothing to enroll in an online account that sends you listings of the properties you are interested in. Have a look.

Chapter 26

CAR BUYING

Here's the one sentence version of this chapter: "Buy the cheapest car you feel safe in." Here's the two sentence version of this chapter: "Buy the cheapest car you feel safe in. Pay cash." Here's the three sentence version of this chapter: "Buy the cheapest car you feel safe in. Pay cash. Shop around."

At the end of it all, you don't need to know too much more than this. There are other, smaller, tips, such as:

- **Buy a car on a Tuesday or Wednesday.** These tend to be the slowest days at a dealership. The slower the day, the more likely the salesperson is going to cut you a deal.

- **Buy a car that is 2 to 5 years old.** The Runzheimer Foundation (that's how you spell it, don't ask me to pronounce it) has done study after study on the ideal "age" of a used car. Even factoring in the cost of additional repairs and expired warranties that can plague used cars, the sweet spot seems to be a car somewhere between 2-5 years old.

- **Check the value at www.kbb.com or www.edmunds.com.** These sites price all sorts of autos of all sorts of ages and mileages. This is especially useful when negotiating with either a dealer or former owner.

- **Find a senior citizen (even if you are a senior citizen).** Seniors tend to have cars with very low mileage. They aren't commuting every day, and they certainly are not drag racing their friends on Friday night (or at least none that I have heard of). Remember that cars are priced on *both* age and mileage. An old car with very little mileage is a great bargain and most likely the senior citizen who is within rock throwing distance of your house has one.

- **Don't let everyone pull your credit.** Car salespeople want to be sure that you can actually afford the car, before they spend 30 minutes trying to sell it to you. So they check your credit report to be sure you would qualify for a loan. But recall from Chapter 13 that pulling your credit in a hard inquiry results in your credit score going down. Better to print your own report out (with the score) and show that to the dealer. Only let the person you eventually buy from check your credit. Try www.creditkarma.com to get a free report and score.

- **Don't just shop the car, shop the financing.** Car dealers aren't the only ones who can lend you money. You can shop their offer at a bank. And you can shop the bank's offer at another bank. And you can shop that bank's offer at a *credit union,* which, as you know, is a nonprofit bank.

- **Monthly payment means NOTHING.** Let me say that again, because this one really pisses me off: Monthly payments mean NOTHING. Car salespeople always want to talk about monthly payments. If you tell them what you can afford each month, they will get you in the car you want to be in, for that monthly payment. What they *don't* tell you is how many months you will be making that payment or what the interest rate will be. Think in terms of total price of the car, a price compared to what you read about in Edmunds or Kelly's Blue Book. (www.edmunds and www.kbb.com)

- **Don't lease.** Unless you are self-employed, this rarely makes sense. There are occasionally gaps in the planetary alignment when leasing can make sense (when a dealer can't sell a particular year or model of car, they offer lease terms so generous that not even the strictest financial advisors can say no). While these deals are out there, they are rare. I am, at the time of this writing however, living proof that they do exist.

- **Forget the extended warranties.** Statistically speaking, they will not pay for themselves. (If they did, automakers couldn't sell them.) Yes, yes, there is always a guy who can tell the story of how the extended warranty saved him at 97,000 miles. Believe it or not, I'm that guy. At 94,000 miles, one of my shocks snapped, puncturing the tire and resulting in $3,000 worth of damage. But thanks to my extended warranty, I paid only $500. So yes, occasionally they pay off. Statistically, however, they do not.

- **You are not your car.** The most dangerous person in the car buying process is *you*. Cars have become a reflection of who we are and how successful we are. I do know people with BMWs who live with their parents, and I know (or at least read about) Sam Walton who, when he was the richest man in America, drove a pickup.[71] Let's be honest, how many of us get swindled by car salespeople and how many of us swindle ourselves?

You can always do something

After my speeches, audience members, upon discovering I have written two (now three) books, ask me, "I've always wanted to write a book. How did you do it?" They are expecting me to say something like, "I just wrote a page a day," or "It's all about discipline." But instead, I tell them the truth, "I had the same car for ten years." Puzzled, they want me to explain. I tell them that by not having to make expensive car payments, I was able to save more money than the average person, thereby able to take more vacation time than the average person (often unpaid vacation time) thereby giving me the time to write my books. Are you *sure* you want that new car?

---

71   This is the dude who founded Walmart.

Chapter 27

YOUR CAREER

This isn't a career book, it's a personal finance book, so I only have one chapter on your career. But for most people, including me, our jobs are our number one source of income. Therefore, they are our number one investment, and we need to do everything in our power to protect it, prosper from it, and since it consumes more than half of our life, hopefully enjoy it.

You protect your job by insuring it with disability insurance like we discussed in Chapter 11. You prosper from your job by taking advantage of all the perks it offers. These "perks" could be anything from a 401k retirement plan with matching contributions from your employer, to discounted coffee in the cafeteria. Whatever it is, not taking advantage of all the perks is the equivalent of handing back a slice of your paycheck.

And speaking of paychecks, here is a bold question to ask (especially in the midst of a recession): *Are you charging what you are worth?* Often times the simplest way to increase your net worth is to ask. I realize that as most people read this, they are going to fight me. They are going to say something like:

- "Pete, my company laid off 30% of its employees, how am I supposed to then go in and ask for a raise?"

- "Pedro, we are on a salary freeze! I can't get a raise on a salary freeze."

- "P Diddy, I have been unemployed for 2 *years*! I just want a freaking job. Whatever they are paying, I'll take."

I hear ya. And I am not suggesting you storm into your boss's office, throw your feet on her desk and say, "I'm overdue for a raise and we both know it." I don't suggest that in any economy.

But remember, you can always do something, so first pull out your goal sheet(s) and your net worth statement. If you are not making what you need to make, figure out how far away you are. Imagine you are currently employed and you earn $50,000 a year. Your company has a salary freeze and a hiring freeze. It's even forbidden to play freeze tag. But you *really* want to earn $55,000 a year. Here's what you do:

Make an appointment with your boss. Tell her what your goals are. Tell her the salary you are trying to achieve. And also reassure her you are completely aware of the present economy, completely aware of the current hiring freeze and salary freeze. And then ask this question:

"What do I need to do to earn $55,000 a year?"

You have now made your salary your boss's problem. If she counters with something to the effect of, "Well, we can talk about pay increases once the salary freeze is over," then you can politely remind her that you didn't ask for a raise. You didn't ask for any money at all. You simply asked her to identify what action on your part would be valuable enough to the company that they would consider paying you more money.

If she is still flustered, prod her with suggestions: "If I brought in 10 new accounts, would that do it?" "If I figured a way to save 10% off all our shipping costs, would that do it?"

I admit, this might not work. But the worst thing that can happen is that your boss would know you are A) goal oriented B) trying to think of ways to save or make the company more money. She can hardly be upset about that.

Also keep in mind that companies have many things to hand out besides paychecks. How about the ability to work from home on Fridays? Or to come in at 10 and leave at 6, thereby ducking all the traffic? How about requesting to be assigned to a more interesting project or sent to a convention that just so happens to be in Hawaii?

But what if I am unemployed?

The unemployed can do this as well. Rather than asking, "Can I have a job?" ask the bigger question, "What do I need to do to work here?" If the company you are interviewing with gives you the standard, "I'm sorry but we are not hiring right now," politely respond, "No worries, I am actually not looking for a job." Tell them you are interested in hearing about their problems and how you can help solve them, on a contingency basis.

What I mean is, stop marketing yourself as an out-of-work person with a set of skills who is looking for a job. Instead, market yourself as an independent consultant who helps companies solve problems on a contingency basis. The contingency is that if you solve their problems, they give you a job.

By taking this approach you can bypass the screeners at human resources altogether because you are not looking for a job. You are in business for yourself, as an independent consultant, so you can go straight to the manager, president or even CEO. Remember, you are *not* looking for a job. You are a problem solver who works on a contingency basis.

If this sounds confusing or unusual, let's take two hypothetical unemployed people. Both were managers of fast food restaurants and both are looking for work in those arenas again.

Patrick tries to find a job the usual way. He puts his resume on the Internet, goes to job fairs, networking events, and hands his information over to a headhunter in his industry. Every morning he wakes up and spends an hour on the web to see what's new.

If he has an interview that day, he shaves and smiles his best smile. If there is a job fair or networking event that night, he attends that, too. But he feels the job fairs have far too many people and far too few booths, and the networking events are really an excuse to drink and be social.

When Patrick does send out a resume to the companies that are hiring, the cover letter looks something like this:

Dear _____,

I saw your ad online for a regional manager for Sloppy Subs. For the past three years, I was the manager at a Barry's Burgers in Denver. As manager, I had only one goal: to be sure every customer had a pleasant and affordable dining experience. I believe my goal was achieved as my restaurant placed first, out of 13, two years in a row in both customer satisfaction reviews and overall sales.

I was in charge of marketing and managing the business as well as hiring and training new employees. My responsibilities also included creating monthly reports, cash flow statements, and maintaining inventory. In 2010, I was awarded "Manager of the Year" by the Denver Restaurant Manager's Association.

I am seeking a full-time management position at a fast food establishment where I can use my skills in marketing, management, and customer service to deliver the same quality experience my Barry's Burgers customers experienced. I have enclosed a resume for your review.

I will be following up next week to arrange an interview.

Sincerely,

Patrick Johnson

Not bad and certainly impressive. I should mention, Patrick is productive with his days. In addition to the job hunting, he has cleaned his apartment and his parent's garage. The bedroom has been painted, much to his girlfriend's delight. Patrick detailed both his car and her car. He reads job interview books at Barnes and Noble and is taking an online course on how to speak Spanish.

But after 18 months, no job.

Brittany, on the other hand, spends just two weeks uploading her resume online and sending it out to headhunters. She, like Patrick, spends an hour every day looking for companies with job postings. She skips the networking events and the job fairs. Aside from the one hour every morning on the Internet, she *does not* look for a job. Instead she looks for problems to solve.

Brittany, like Patrick, works in the fast food industry. But rather than looking at only the companies that are hiring, she looks at *every* company in her area that she wants to work for. Every morning, after the Internet search, she gets in her car and visits one fast food restaurant a day for lunch. She takes her laptop. And she starts to take notes.

She doesn't just visit the franchises. She also visits the small mom and pop operations. She casually chats with customers, wondering why they eat here and not elsewhere. Brittany asks what their favorite meal is. Customers tell her things like, "I eat here because they compost their food, and the big franchises do not." She then asks the manager about how the composting works, and he proudly explains exactly how it is done.

Day after day, week after week, Brittany visits these restaurants. Many days, nothing exciting happens. The restaurants seem to be the same most of the time. But occasionally, like with the composting, she gets a gem. She collects these gems and compiles them into a 50-page report.

She then goes back to her list of companies she wants to work for. Depending on the company, she finds the president, CEO, senior vice president or regional manager. She does *not* look for the head of human resources department, because remember, she is not looking for a job. She is a problem solver.

The New Resume

Since Brittany is not looking for a job, she won't send a resume. So she sends what Jeffery Fox, in his wonderful book, *Don't Send A Resume*, calls an *impact letter*. It reads something like this:

Dear _____

Ever since I moved to New England, I've been a big fan of your Burrito Wagon restaurants. Before coming to the Northeast, I managed a similar restaurant in Texas called Burrito World. I was the only manager in the state of Texas to win Outstanding Manager of the Year 3 years in a row.

During the past 6 weeks, I have visited every one of your restaurants in the greater Boston area. I have also visited 70 of your competitors, both the franchises and the smaller "mom and pop" operations. I've spent my days interviewing customers and managers at all of these establishments and I have summarized my research into a 50-page report.

If you would like a copy, free of charge, I am happy to hand deliver it to your office. I will actually be in your area next week on both Tuesday and Thursday, from 10 a.m. to 4 pm. I would welcome the chance to show you the report and discuss my research. Because I am such a fan, you are the first company I have approached to show the report to.

Even though I have five years experience managing fast food restaurants, I must admit my research surprised me. For example, the senior management at Burrito World always believed that composting was too expensive. I can only conclude your restaurants feel the same way since they don't partake in it. But I found a unique, out-of-the-way burger joint that not only composts, but also <u>profits</u> from it. When we meet, I'll tell you all about it.

My Best,

Brittany Spars[72]

Now you tell me: Who is going to get a job first? Sure, the manager could be thinking, "Yeah, we already looked into composting, and it didn't work." If that's the kind of manager he is, then Brittany doesn't want to work for him anyway. She, like you, doesn't want to work for *anyone* who doesn't appreciate her ideas, talents and suggestions. Period.

More likely however, these are the thoughts running through the manager's head:

---

72 This is the name that popped into my head, and I'm sticking with it.

"Composting huh? Yeah we did look at that, but maybe this girl found something we didn't."

- "She's gonna *give* me this report for free? Wait, who *else* is she going to hand deliver the report to? The letter says that Burrito World is first company she approached. If I ignore her, she might approach someone else."

- "What do I have to lose by meeting with her? So she tries to sell me something? So what? I meet with salespeople all the time."

- And probably the most prominent thing running through the manager's mind was, "Wait wait wait. This girl spent her *free time* writing this report? I want someone like that working for me. I don't care if human resources says we're not hiring. We're hiring *her*."

Is this out of the box? Sure. And feel free to keep posting your resumes online and applying only to companies that claim to be hiring. But after 12 months of that, it's time for something bolder. It's time to do what no one else is doing and look where no one else is looking.

TRUE STORY

Many years ago, I was dating a woman who hit me with the grim sentence, "We need to talk." "I'm not ready for a boyfriend," she told me. "I want my freedom." Of course, I was hurt, but I appreciated her honesty, and we agreed to just be friends.[73]

Two weeks later, I discovered she had a boyfriend and was in a serious relationship, the very kind she told me she *didn't* want. "WTF?" I asked my friend. "She told me she didn't want a boyfriend. What the hell happened in two weeks?"

"Peter," my friend said, "she *did* want a boyfriend. She just didn't want you." Ouch. But he was right. He hit me on the chin with it, but he was right.

---

73 And by "friends" I mean we never spoke again.

And now dear reader, I need to hit you on the chin by saying that _any_ company, will hire _anyone_, at _any_ time, for _any_ position, if that person can prove they can make the company more money than they will cost them. Companies "purchase" employees for the same reason they purchase new computer software; because it will save them or make them more money.

Sending out a bunch of resumes doesn't prove anything except that you are looking for a job. Start looking for problems to solve, figure out how to solve them, and share those ideas with companies. Do this enough, and someone will see the value.

You can always do something

If you have tried all the usual stuff – career fairs, HotJobs, Monster.com – it's time to try something different like what Brittany did with her report and impact letter. Bold, indeed, but bold is where you go when the other stuff doesn't work.

Part 4
The Weird Stuff

BY NOW, WE'VE COVERED MOST OF THE ESSENTIAL STUFF IN PERSONAL FINANCE. NOW IT'S TIME TO GO OFF THE BEATEN PATH, TO THE STUFF YOU HAVEN'T HEARD BEFORE. OR IF YOU HAVE HEARD THE STUFF BEFORE, LIKE GOLD AND SILVER, IT'S TIME TO LOOK AT IT IN A NEW LIGHT. NOT EVERY CHAPTER IS ABOUT AN INVESTMENT, AND THE INVESTMENTS THAT ARE DISCUSSED HERE AREN'T FOR EVERYONE. BUT IT NEVER HURTS TO THINK OUTSIDE THE FINANCIAL BOX. HERE WE GO.

Chapter 28

GOLD: A HISTORY LESSON

WTF is everyone talking about gold?

For over 6,000 years, gold has been used as a form of currency. It does not rust, it is difficult to create a forgery, there is a limited supply of it, and we can only get that supply at a certain rate. To be an established currency for more than 6,000 years is pretty impressive; and gold has enjoyed those bragging rights because of the qualities described above.

Investors, even gold investors (affectionately referred to as the Gold Bugs), actually don't like owning gold. In two words: Gold sucks. You have to pay to store it, insure it, and if you want to hold it, you have to pay shipping. Gold pays no interest or dividends. Short selling aside, you can only make money if the price goes up.[74]

The price of gold is determined by market demand and supply. Thankfully (well, unless you're a gold miner), the supply has remained steady for the past 2,000 years. We can only get it out of the ground so fast, and this speed has kept pace with the demand. There are mining companies that have *literally* been sitting on a gold mine and have chosen not to extract the gold, simply because the digging is too expensive based on current prices. When the price gets high enough, only then will they break out the hard hats and shovels.

So we are unlikely to see a mining company dump a bajillion tons of gold onto the gold markets. Instead, market demand is going to make the price of gold rise and fall.

---

74   Remember short selling or "shorting" is a way to make money when an investment - stocks, gold etc. - goes *down*. It's risky because it is one of the few investment strategies with *unlimited* loss.

Gold has one unique quality and that is that it has an *intrinsic* value. It is always worth *something*. Granted, real estate has this as well, but we often buy real estate with debt, which makes this a moot point. Gold has never gone, and never will go, to zero. Can't say the same for Penn Central.[75]

People typically buy gold when there is bad news out there. When unemployment is high or when the stock or real estate markets crash, gold becomes the safety net. Recently however, folks have been buying gold because of a heightened skepticism in the US Dollar.

The US Dollar has had an interesting history, which I don't have the pages or the patience to recite. So I will give you the short version. BTW if you have a buck in your pocket, take it out. I think you'll find this interesting.

- If you walked into a bank in 1912, slapped a $50 on the counter and said "Pay up!" What would happen? The banker would legally have to give you $50 in gold coins. This is because it reads, right on that $50 bill, these words: *"United States Of America $50 In Gold Coin Payable to the Bearer on demand."* You're the bearer, and you demand your money. When a government keeps an amount of gold in storage equal to the amount of paper money in circulation, that government is known to be on a *gold standard*. We used to be, now we are not. And neither is anyone else.[76]

- If you walked into a bank today, slapped a $50 on the counter and said "Pay up!" the banker would say, "And how would you like that? In fives and tens?" If you glanced down at your $50 bill (or the $1 bill you are holding now) you would read these words: *"This Note Is Legal Tender For All Debts Public And Private."*

We have come a long way, from being a country whose dollars were backed by gold, to having what is known as a *fiat* currency, which means nothing backs the currency except the law. If a business is selling shirts for $20 and you hand over a $20 bill, they *must* accept that $20 bill as payment. Otherwise they are breaking the law.[77]

---

75 Ahhh good ole' Penn Central. Google it.
76 Yep. The Swiss gave this up at the turn of the millennium. They were the last.
77 Can you *really* go to prison for not accepting US Dollars as payment? Yes! You go to the same jail where they keep the people who cut the tags off mattresses.

Since our dollars are backed by nothing, the Federal Reserve can legally print as many dollars as it wants, thereby increasing the *money supply*. Typically they avoid doing this because too many dollars makes the value of each dollar worth less. It's like having a rare baseball card worth $100,000 and then some jerk in Iowa suddenly finds a boxful of these cards in his grandfather's closet. The value of your card has gone down because it is not as rare.

So too with dollars. The more they print, the less each one is worth. The trouble is, under *both* Democrat and Republican presidents, the printing presses have been a crankin'! When this happens, people get nervous. It's not so much that prices rise, it's that dollars are worth less, so you need more dollars to buy the same stuff. This is called *inflation*.

To hedge against this, people buy gold, which will rise with the prices of all the other stuff. The decade-long rise in gold has mainly to do with the rising number of dollars in circulation. Recently, gold has spiked because added to the abnormal abundance of dollars has been high unemployment, a jittery stock market and a mortgage crisis.

Soooooo … when does gold go down? Historically, in uncertain times such as these, gold keeps going up until we arrive at a de facto gold standard. This is kinda like a gold standard by default. What happens is, the price of gold gets high enough to match the amount of US dollars in existence. Confused? Me too.

Imagine there was only *one* ounce of gold in all of America. The current market price of that gold is $20 an ounce. Also pretend that until last week, there were only 50 $1 bills in existence. But last week, the government printed another 50 $1 bills. The total money supply is now $100 (a hundred $1 bills). Because of the government's recent printing, the price of that one gold coin starts to creep up and up.

History tells us that gold will "peak" when the value of the gold coin matches the number of dollars in circulation. In our simple example here, that would mean a gold price of $100 an ounce. When they match, we are essentially on a temporary gold standard, where every dollar is accounted for by an amount of gold.

In the real world, gold experts believe this "match up" price is currently somewhere between $3,000 and *$15,000* an ounce.[78] The number of US Dollars in circulation – the money supply – has gotten so large that the price of gold has to go this high. (Or at least this is their argument.)

Before we draw the curtain on this chapter, I need to quickly discuss gold's dirty little secret. And that is gold's historic last minute binge and subsequent hangover. Gold does keep rising until it gets near or at the de facto gold standard mentioned above. That is true. But what people fail to realize is that historically gold tends to do this very quickly and come down even quicker.

In the last gold rush of the late 1970s, gold hit $850 an ounce in 1980. But just a year before that peak, it was trading around *half* that value. A year later, gold lost *half* its 1980 peak value. In short, it was one hell of a roller coaster ride, and it all happened *very* quickly. So even if the gold bugs are right about precious metals – that they will go much, much higher – investors need to be careful because metals crash very fast once they hit their peak.

Scared? Don't be. In the next chapter, I will tell you how to kinda sorta never lose money in precious metals.

You can always do something

This was the gold crash course. Gold sucks as an investment since we have to pay to ensure it and store it, and it pays no dividends. However our current economic situation warrants that precious metals get a closer look. So increase your education on gold. Try the website www.goldsilver.com, which has a lot of free videos. (They sell gold and silver, but the videos are good.) Also, turn the page for a cool way to invest in precious metals.

---

78   As I write this, gold floats around $1,700 an ounce.

Chapter 29

HOW TO KINDA SORTA NEVER
LOSE MONEY IN PRECIOUS METALS

There are many precious metals you can buy, with gold, silver, platinum, and palladium being the most popular. Unless you are buying them through a precious metals fund, I would forget all of them – even gold – and stick with silver. Here's why.

Remember how I told you in the last chapter companies are sitting on gold mines waiting to be dug up? The worldwide gold supply has remained steady. The worldwide silver supply, on the other hand, is going *down*. We are using it up faster than we can dig it out of the ground. Silver is not just found in jewelry and coins, it's also in many of our electronics and everyday household items. Items such as windows, flat screen TVs and, of course, silverware, all contain silver. With the other metals, recycling is worth it. Not so with silver. That's why we are running out of it.

So the supply of silver is going down and the current market uncertainty is forcing silver to go up in price. But just like gold, silver can come crashing down just as fast. So if you own a bunch of it, you still could be out of luck.

Unless ...

Remember in Chapter 20 when I revealed ten important questions to ask yourself before you buy an investment? The first being *what else would I buy?* Well, I'd like you to start asking that same question, only I want you to start asking it in an area outside of your financial life. I want you to ask it every time you are about to buy someone a gift, and I would like you to consider answering with the word "silver."

Think about all the people you have to buy presents for. Your kids. Niece. Nephew. Your brothers and/or sisters. Cousins. Friends. Your doorman, mailman, hairdresser or landscaper. Now think of all the events you have to buy gifts for these people for. Christmas. Chanukah. Birthdays. Graduation. Weddings. Bridal showers. Baby showers. Flag Day.

And now think, just for a moment, about all the *crap* you have given and gotten over the years. Pile on top of that all the frustration you have undergone trying to find the right gifts at the last minute. What size is your niece? That video game your cousin asked for, what was it called again? Did you notice that toy castle you bought your nephew a year ago never gets played with anymore?

Suppose next year you had to buy gifts for three cousins, one brother, three weddings and one new born. Your brother and cousins need gifts on their birthdays and on Christmas, and one of your cousins is graduating college. Imagine you want to spend $100 on each of the wedding gifts, $50 on the graduation and newborn gifts, and $30 on every other gift. In total you are going to blow $580 on gifts. Or to put it more bluntly, you are going to *lose* $580 this year and most likely in subsequent years by buying people stuff they don't need.

Suppose, instead, you committed to buying one ounce Silver American Eagle coins (currently valued at around $30). If the silver market goes up, feel free to keep the coins and not give them away as gifts. If the market crashes, then you haven't "lost" anything because it's money you would have had to spend on a gift. Just give the coins as gifts. That's why I called this Chapter How to Kinda Sorta Never Lose Money in Precious Metals.[79]

My snootier readers will claim it is rude to give money as a gift. Or it is thoughtless to use your friends as a hedge against the silver market. I disagree. Thoughtlessness is running through the mall, pushing senior citizens out of the way because you're having dinner at your brother's house and it's his wife's birthday and you forgot. (Now where the hell is that thoughtless-scented-candle-store?)

And how is it rude to give money but not rude to give each other

---

[79] What happens when the price of a 1 ounce coin goes to $100 and you want to give someone a $30 gift? You can buy half ounce coins and 1/10th of an ounce coins, so no worries.

crap? The last Yankee Swap I participated in, I found myself the proud owner of a tool set from one of the big box stores (not that one, the other one). A week later, the tip of the screwdriver in that box *broke* off. Six weeks later, under a barrage of curses, I threw the *entire* toolbox into the dumpster. Half the tools in the box had become useless because of their horrendously poor quality. Yet because it looked good in a box, it was considered a nice gesture.

Let's stop giving each other crap and *start* giving each other value. If you have young children, grandchildren, nieces and nephews, you and I both know that all the toys you buy them this year will be taking up space in a landfill within three years. Silver coins will *never* have a zero value, and a hatful of these coins, built up over the years, will truly mean something when they turn eighteen.

You can always do something

This section is all about alternative strategies to help you overcome your fear of doing anything. People are nervous about investing in precious metals. Here's a way to not have to worry about it. And if you fall into that snooty category opposed to giving silver as a gift, I remind you that to improve our economy, we *all* must make a cultural change. To constantly buy cheap manufactured goods might make China rich, but it delays our long-term prosperity.

Chapter 30

USING LIFE INSURANCE AS A BANK

This isn't for everyone.

We discussed life insurance in Chapter 11 from the obvious perspective: as life insurance. However, whole life insurance can be used for a variety of different things. It can be used as a tax shelter to save money, or as collateral to get a loan from a bank. But perhaps most interesting of all is the strategy on how to use whole life insurance as a bank. To understand this, let's first talk about how banks work.

Deposit $1,000 into the bank and the bank pays you 1% annual interest on that $1,000. But that money doesn't stay in the vault. About 80%-90% of it gets lent out to someone else at, say, 6%. The bank makes its profit on the difference between collecting money at 6% and paying you use of that money at 1%. In a weird way, your money is in *two* places at once: 1) sitting in the vault paying you 1% *and* 2) in the hands of whoever borrowed it at 6%. Sounds like a good deal huh? *Yeah, for the bank.*

You can do the same thing, however, with whole life insurance. Now if you read most financial books, or even my book *Getting Loaded,* you will see financial authors agree that for most households, term life insurance is the better bet. It's about 1/10 the price of whole life, it's difficult to get ripped off, and the commissions are pretty small.

However, we of the financial education world are referring to 95% of whole life policies when we give the above advice. That is to say, many of the policies are laden with heavy commissions, and too many salespeople put their needs above your own. Were you to find a salesperson who has a long-term outlook on his or her business and had the ability to see life insurance in a different light, rather than beating you up for the commissions, you might be able to use a whole life policy as a bank. The good news is that I not only found one of these salespeople, I actually found two. But more on them in a minute. First, let me explain how this actually works.

Whole life insurance, as you now know, allows you to build up a cash value. When you pay a $1,000 annual premium on a whole life policy, some of that money goes to pay the cost of insurance, but some of it goes into an account that pays a guaranteed minimum amount of interest.

The interesting thing is that you can borrow against the money in your policy. You do however have to pay interest for this, just as you would on a normal loan. The good news is that when you borrow money out of your whole life insurance policy, you pay an interest rate for only the amount you borrow, but you *get paid* on the *full* amount of the policy. Like a bank, your money is in two places at once.

Confused? I certainly was when I first heard it. So let's try an example. Suppose your whole life insurance policy currently has a $20,000 cash value. Suppose also that the policy pays you a guaranteed 4% per year in interest. Now suppose you want to borrow $10,000 to go on a trip. Your policy allows you to borrow that money at 6% per year. So you call up your life insurance agent and say send me $10,000. She does, and that $10,000 is now in your pocket and it costs you $600 a year ($10,000 x 6%) in interest to borrow it. Eventually you'll have to pay the $10,000 back, but that is at your leisure.

But remember, like a bank, your money is in two places at once. Even though your policy technically only has $10,000 in it, because you took half of it out in the form of a loan, the policy *still* pays you 4% on the *full* $20,000. So you earn $800 a year off the policy. Half the money is in your pocket, but you still get paid on *all* of it.

Okay, so how would you use this? Well imagine you were going to buy a car for $20,000. You have four options to buy that car:

1. **You could lease it.**

2. **You could buy it outright using $20,000.**

3. **You could get a loan for $20,000, say at 6% interest from either the bank or the car dealer.**

4. **Or you could borrow money from your whole life insurance policy.**

Leasing is essentially a loan. The interest on a lease is built into the payments. Plus you never end up owning the car. If you paid cash, you would no longer be able to earn any interest off that $20,000 in the bank; this is what economists call opportunity cost. If you were to borrow the money, you would pay interest.

With a whole life policy, you would still have to pay interest, but you would also be earning interest on the face value of the policy. So if you simply agreed to borrow the money at 6% from your whole life policy and pay *yourself* back that 6%, you would have been earning 4% the whole time the money was being paid back.[80]

Utterly confused? Then I have done my job. But all jokes aside, this is one of those out of the box strategies, especially for those folks who have become very wary about the stock market. Remember you can always do something, and using whole life insurance as a bank is an interesting "something." Not to mention, doing this also provides you with at least some of the life insurance you will need.

While many life insurance salespeople will claim to offer these policies, the truth is many of them do not specialize in this type of insurance. The policy is a very specific one, so be sure you are working with someone who has done this before. I can steer you toward two people who specialize in this. As always, I receive no commission or referral fee from suggesting them:

---

80   You could of course achieve this by leaving your $20,000 in the bank and getting a bank loan, but currently banks are paying around 1%, while life insurance companies are paying around 4%, with the borrowing rates roughly the same. Dividends in a life insurance policy are also protected from taxes.

- Pamela Yellen: Bank On Yourself www.bankonyourself.com
- Walter Young: Fortiphi Financial www.fortiphi.com

You can always do something

If you want to dabble outside of the box, check out these websites. Call them up. I do have one of these policies myself, and over the long term, they can be a unique and lucrative way to build wealth.

Chapter 31

HOW TO BEAT THE STOCK MARKET

No way!

Yes way!

The cool thing about plagiarizing is if you announce, publically, that you are about to plagiarize then it is no longer plagiarizing, it's called *quoting*. I confess to not being the guy who invented this formula for beating the market, I only confess to plag– ... I mean quoting it. The guy I will be quoting is Joel Greenblatt, whose firm, Gotham Capital,[81] had an annualized return of 40% for 20 years beginning in 1985. In short, he kicked ass.

Joel – excuse me, Mr. Greenblatt – developed a formula that appears to beat the market and appears it will keep doing so, even if nearly everybody starts using it. (Unlike other formulas, which once they get too popular, they lose their ability to outperform the averages.) The biggest downside to Mr. Greenblatt's formula has nothing to do with Monsieur Greenblatt, or his formula, but *you*.

Yes you, dear reader. The formula I am about to describe doesn't work every year, but over time it beats the market – and it appears it will continue to do so. But if it lets you down for a year or two or three, you will probably abandon it. No offense, I would do the same thing. I'd get pissed off it wasn't working, and I would try something else. Doing so, history tells us, would be costly.

---

81 Batman was the CEO of Gotham Capital, and Robin was Chief Financial Officer. Supposedly one employee was fired for being a real Joker, and another was apparently let go for being Two-Face(d).

So what's the formula? Well hold on. First let me explain *why* it works. Grab ye' any financial newspaper and turn to the pages that have the stock quotes, or look them up online. You will see, listed next to each company is not only its current share price, but also the 52 week high and low share price. Find some of the big brand name companies you know and love. Notice the *huge* market swings between the 52-week high and low.

What's going on here? Is McDonald's selling twice as many hamburgers during its 52 high and half as many during its 52-week low? Of course not. As you learned in Chapter 21, the price of a stock is influenced by the number of buyers and sellers. But WTF are these buyers and sellers thinking? The companies can't change *that* much. Probably not, but for whatever reason, either fear or greed, people drive prices way up or down. This tells us that in the *short term*, the stock market is *irrational*.

But good companies with sound financials survive. They do not go bankrupt. Sure, there will be some surprises, but in the *long term*, the stock market is *rational*. So if you can identify these good companies, and then buy them when their price is low, you should be rewarded as the market moves from the short term, irrational, state of ignoring them to the long term, rational, state of buying them.

Normally, this is the part where I say, "but that's easier said than done, folks." And I used to, until I read Mr. Greenblatt's book, *The Little Book That Beats the Market.* It does live up to its name. It is little, it is indeed a book, and it does beat the market using a simple formula that has just a few steps:

1. Rank the top 3,500 U.S. stocks based on their return on capital.[82]

2. Then rank the top 3,500 U.S. stocks based on their earnings yield.[83]

3. Then find the companies that rank high on *both* lists, by adding their positions together. So if Microsoft ranks 12 on List #1 and 457th on List #2, Microsoft's combined rank is 469th (12 + 457).

---

82 Huh? Return on capital is how much money a company makes off the money it invests in itself. So if a French fry company invests $1,000 in an auto fry slicer that saves them $300 a year, that's a 30% return on capital. The higher this number, the better.
83 Wha? Earnings yield is a comparison of how much a company is earning compared to its price. A high earnings yield means the company is selling for cheap *while* earning a lot of money.

4. Buy the top 30 ranking companies based on their combined rank.

5. Readjust once a year.

Bam! That's it. *La fin* as they say in whatever language they say that in. Confused? Still too much work? Mr. Greenblatt has generously created a website with the corny title www.magicformulainvesting.com. Here's the kicker: *It's free!* The site helps you find the stocks. Easy!

You can always do something

Don't follow this blindly. I gave you the crash course version of the crash course version of Mr. Greenblatt's course. Read his book *The Little Book That Beats the Market.* Seriously, read it. Then visit www.magicformulainvesting.com and have a look around. If it makes sense to you, consider trying it with 10% of your portfolio. Commit to it for at least five years. If it's working, you can increase the percentage of your portfolio. You also can start bragging.

Chapter 32

STUPID STUFF I'VE DONE

Admittedly, this would fill a separate book. So I will limit it to only the financial stuff, leaving out stuff like the time I forgot to make dinner reservations on Valentine's Day.[84] Also in the interests of brevity, I will limit it to only the *dumbest* stuff. So without further ado, I have:

- Gotten into lots of credit card debt.

- Gotten into lots of credit card debt after I had dug myself out of credit card debt years earlier.

- Paid more than 60 days late on a credit card because I didn't have the money.

- Bounced a check. Or two. Or twelve.

- Put the phone bill in my name while living with a roommate I didn't know. Some $2,000 later, I knew a lot about him, most interesting of which was that he had a girlfriend in South America.

- Taken a cash advance on a credit card (when the banker himself warned me not to do this).

- At times, screwed up my business. The first year of my speaking business I had a net loss of $5,000. Frustrated, I vowed in the second year, to get organized, work harder, work smarter, market better, and cut costs. I lost $12,000.

- Attended a convention, heard a guy mention what he thought was a hot stock, immediately bought $1,500 worth of it that night. I sold it for $300 two weeks later.

---

84   What? I thought we would be able to walk right in and get a table.

- Bought a house with 100% financing, part of which was an adjustable rate loan.

- Paid $5,000 to a business consultant who promised to get me an infomercial for my products. Haven't seen it yet have ya? Neither have I.

- Left a relationship with a woman I really enjoyed because I was ashamed at the time that I wasn't making enough money. (This one really hurt.)

- Listened for *years* to people who told me my business would never work and therefore delayed even starting it.

- Took money out of a retirement account early and paid the 10% penalty. (Yeah yeah, I know, I know.)

Shall I go on? No need. I bring all this up to reveal that I have done plenty of stupid stuff, even after I read about how stupid doing such stuff is.

You can always do something

I have made a great many financial mistakes. Even as someone who is well educated in the realm of personal finance and tries to serve as a role model, I *continue* to do stupid stuff. Sometimes I am being greedy, sometimes I am being fearful, and most times I am just being a moron. I'm human. So are you. Life happens. Move on from your mistakes. Focus on the big picture and remember: *You can always do something.*

Chapter 33

COMMON MISCONCEPTIONS

1. **You write checks to the IRS.** Nope. The IRS is nothing more than a collection agency. They do not write the rules, and they do not get to keep any of the tax money. Your tax payments go to the U.S. Treasury, and Congress gets to decide where to spend it.

2. **If I buy a house with a fixed-rate loan, my payments will never go up.** Ahhh, this one got a lot of people into trouble. A true fixed-rate home loan will not have its payments increase. But the loan is only one cost to owning a home. Taxes and insurance can (and always do) go up. So if your "fixed" monthly payment started out as $2,000 a month and went up, it was probably due to an insurance or tax increase. Repairs can also spring up at any time.

3. **You pay off a mortgage.** People always say this, but it is actually not true. You pay off a *loan*. The mortgage is the legal instrument that attaches your house to your loan. If you cannot pay the loan, the lender can take your house. When an asset (a house, a business etc.) is attached to a loan, it is called a *secured* loan. Unsecured loans, like credit cards, do not allow the lender to automatically take anything from you. They must first take you to court and get a judgment.

4. **The stock market is nothing more than legalized gambling.** Not true. Most casino games are driven by luck. The roll of the dice cannot be influenced by anything you do. Indeed, if you are smart enough, you can count cards in blackjack, but now many casinos are using automatic shuffle machines, so the decks are

continuous.[85] In the stock market, you can make money purchasing great companies before the crowds – either through genuine ignorance or outright delusion – realize they are great. When the crowds buy in, your stock price will go up. You can also buy *everything*, realizing that the losers can only go to zero and that the winners have no limit. One cannot do this on a roulette wheel and come out ahead.

5. **I am married, so my spouse and I now have a merged credit report.** Nope. You will always have your own. If you buy a house together, then your mortgage broker will average your two scores. But for the rest of your life, you will always have your own credit report and score.

6. **Peter Bielagus is the best financial writer in the country.** Alas, he is not. The best financial writer in the country is a gent named Andrew Tobias. I'm talking pure word smithery here, but this guy's gift with words is unsurpassed in the financial community. He would never make up a word like "smithery." His book, *The Only Investment Guide You'll Ever Need* was the first financial book I ever read, and it taught me that A) finance isn't as complicated as everyone thinks and B) finance can be fun.

You can always do something

Financial misconceptions arise because people don't take the time to understand their investments. Slow down and be sure you get it, before you venture into it.

---

85 Although I was just in Vegas and was surprised to see the return of one deck blackjack. This is due mainly to the economy.

Chapter 34

QUESTIONS I GET ALL THE TIME BUT I HATE ANSWERING

My son/daughter doesn't seem to care about managing their money. What can I say to motivate them? I give a lot of speeches to parents, and this one always comes up. Often the key is not to say something new, but to *stop* saying what you have been saying. Parents, grandparents, aunts, uncles, even teachers often say things like:

- "Oh to, be young again."
- "I remember when I was your age."
- "This is the time of your life."
- "Enjoy it while it lasts."
- "Wait till you get to the real world."

Often these are harmless statements, meant as a joke. The trouble is they have a devastating effect. What these comments telegraph to a young person is that life gets more and more difficult. So why not party now and pay for it later? Instead, try to convey that with proper financial planning, life does get better year after year. It gets easier to pay for your personal life.

My other tip here is to stop focusing on what your kids *should* do and start focusing on what they *will* do. If I had my way, I would spend my college speeches talking about disability insurance. It is by far the most overlooked component of a financial plan. But I don't utter a word about it. Why? Because it's *boring*. Instead I focus a lot on credit scores, because they are sexy and because college students understand the concept of having their lives reduced to one number.[86]

Start teaching the most exciting part of personal finance to your child. This could be credit scores, investing in stocks or starting their own business. Then, when their interest is peaked (and it may take a while) eventually they will wander to all the other important areas of personal finance.

My parents are getting up there in age. What am I supposed to say to them, and how do I say it without being insensitive? Your parents need an estate plan, like we discussed in Chapter 16. They also need to know where they will live in their golden years and how they are going to pay for it. I agree this can be a tough subject to bring up, and many baby boomers don't want to talk about it.

The way around this is to ask, suggest, and if necessary, *force* your parents to see a *fee-only*[87] financial planner. This is someone who does not sell any investments or make any commissions. They charge a flat hourly rate to listen to your situation and provide their advice. Depending on where you live and what your financial life looks like, that will be somewhere in the neighborhood of $500-$2,500, but worth every penny. The financial planner's job is not to be nice but to be blunt. They'll say all the things you wish you could. Let them handle it.

I am about to get married, what should I ask my future schnookie bums? Before you take el plunge with that special someone there are three things you need to discuss:

1. Credit scores

2. Goals

3. The pre nup

Credit Scores: Remember, you don't have merged credit reports, but if you are planning on moving into an apartment, buying a house or car together, then what's on his/her credit report will affect yours. Cook a romantic dinner, grab a couple glasses of red wine, and then visit annualcreditreport.com. Show each other whatcha got.

---

86   Because of the SAT, the LSAT, the MCAT, etc.
87   No no. Not fee-*based*, not a financial "consultant," *a fee only* planner. For suggestions in your area visit www.napfa.org.

I am not saying only date people with good credit.[88] You simply need to know a lot of things about your significant other, and this is one of them.

Goals: I am shocked at how many couples don't share their goals. If you truly want to be a stay-at-home dad so you can finish the Great American Novel, you need to tell your spouse you will quit the law firm the moment the opportunity arrives. If you want to delay having kids so you can get your business off the ground, you need to share that too. If nice cars are important to you, fess up. Take the goal sheet from Chapter 3 and fill it out. Share that with your soon to be spouse. If your goals are too far apart, find areas where you and schnookie bums can make some tradeoffs.

Pre nup: Yep, you need one. "But our relationship is different," you say? About 55% of married couples said the same thing, and they ended in divorce. You can skip this step – I really want to when I meet the future Mrs. Bielagus – but statistically speaking, it should be done. If you are nervous about bringing it up (and who wouldn't be), you can make an appointment with a fee-only financial advisor, and they will bring it up. They'll also tell you what it should include.

I am married, what should I say to my spouse?[89] Money management issues are the number one reason couples get divorced. It is important to keep sharing what your goals are if they change. Maybe you always wanted to be a high-powered corporate woman, but holding your tiny son in your hands changed all that. Maybe after four years of 100-hour work weeks at the law firm, you realize that no amount of money can tempt you to continue. Goals do change, and it's important the communication keep pace with that.

My daughter is $20,000 in credit card debt. I have the means to bail her out, but should I? I really hate this one, but yes. That debt, unless your daughter is expecting a surge in her income, will drastically drag down her ability to become financially free.

This is not to say she gets free money. If her credit card debt is at 18%, consider offering her a loan at 6% for ten years. It's great deal for her, and given current interest rates, it's not such a bad deal for you either. Sign a

---

88 Doing so would annihilate the "plenty of fish in the sea" theory.
89 Besides, "I'm sorry" and "yes dear."

loan contract. Include late fees. Ideally set up an automatic payment plan. Perhaps $100 of her paycheck can be sent directly to you before it touches her hands. Force her to cut up all her credit cards and sit with her three times a year to check her credit. Set up an email alert to remind her 2 days before her payment is due.

Should I pay off my credit card debt faster by *not* contributing to my retirement account? This is all about interest rates. Assume your retirement account is going to earn you about 8%. If your credit cards are *losing* you 15%, then it probably makes sense to hit those a bit harder. The exception is if you are in a very high tax bracket, the deduction for contributing to a retirement account may make it worth it. The other exception would be if your employer matches your contributions, then take advantage of those first. People get all in a tizzy trying to figure out which is best. The truth is doing *either one* will help your financial life, as long as you do it consistently and aggressively. As a rule of thumb, at a minimum you should double the minimum payments on your credit cards. Once you do that, feel free to put the rest to retirement savings.

> As a rule of thumb, at a minimum you should *double* the minimum payments on your credit cards.

Should I pay off my adjustable rate mortgage faster by *not* contributing to my retirement account? Again, it all comes down to interest rates. As I write this, your interest rate on your home loan is probably pretty good. But when you *read* this book, that may not be the case. Again, using 8% as the yardstick for your retirement account, if your home loan reaches above that, it's probably better to get going on the home loan (noting the two exceptions above regarding retirement accounts). But again, either one will improve your financial life.

Should I fund my emergency reserve account first by *not* contributing to my retirement account? Nah. The emergency account is important, but it does not have to be fully funded right away. The one severe drawback to *not* contributing to your retirement accounts is that once the year passes, you lose the opportunity to contribute that year *forever*. The IRS allows no catching up.[90]

Can I borrow against my 401k to payoff credit card debt? How about an adjustable rate home loan? Nope. 401k loans seem cool, but they're not. The reason why is because if you get laid off, many times the loan is *callable*. This means you may have only a few months to pay the whole thing off, otherwise they take your retirement account. If you're really stuck, I'd rather you stop making future contributions than take out a loan.

I owe money to a collection agent but I haven't heard from them in years. Should I just let it go? Ethically, no. My belief is if you borrow money you should pay it back. If you need more time, a lower interest rate, lower payments, or even a settlement where some debt is forgiven, that's all fine. But to ignore it, I do have an issue with that.

The trouble is that sometimes the credit reporting agencies punish you for *paying* an old debt. The "old" activity of an old debt suddenly moves to the beginning of your credit report when you pay it. Remember how in Chapter 13 we discussed that the credit score cares most about what happened in the last 2-3 years? Well, paying an old debt moves it into that zone and can at times bring down your score.

So what's the answer? Remember, with debt collectors you can negotiate not only how much you will pay, when you will pay it, you can also negotiate how they will *report* to the credit bureaus. You could ask for a pay for deletion contract. You could ask that they not report it at all and just let the debt die off (if it's close to 7 years old).

I have a very special purchase that I cannot afford? Can I charge it? Please do! Remember the goal is to achieve your goals, not to have

---

90 Jerks.

more money. I am not going to tell you to skip a honeymoon, or deny your daughter the right to study overseas. Just riddle me this: *What are you willing to give up in order to pay for the new purchase?* No more dinners out? Carpool to work three days a week? Maybe even move to a cheaper apartment?

You can always do something

Knowing the stuff to avoid and clarifying the misnomers is crucial to your financial life. So is communication. Do so many marriages end in divorce because couples don't have enough money or simply because they don't *talk* about money? I think the latter, and if I am right, that problem is easily solved.

Chapter 35

HOW TO PROTECT AGAINST
THE NEXT BERNIE MADOFF

Picture two brothers, Dickey and Clyde. Every Friday on their way to happy hour, they both stop to deposit $1,000 into their brokerage accounts. Clyde deposits his money with Edward Jones[91]. Dickey deposits his money with Madoff Investment Securities LLC.

When Dickey walks into his broker's office, he hands them a $1,000 check, and they hand him a piece of paper that reads he just handed them a $1,000 check. Edward Jones does the exact same thing for Clyde. Each of them gets a paper statement every month describing how much is in their account.

Dickey's returns are usually a little bit better than Clyde's. There are, however, some years that Clyde actually does better than Dickey. Clyde personally knows a few millionaires that invest with Edward Jones. Dickey also personally knows a few millionaires that invest with Madoff's company.

After 10 years of doing this, Clyde and Dickey decide to sell some of their stocks and buy a boat. Both sell $50,000 worth of stock. Five days later, both receive checks from the sale, and both checks cash.

How then is one supposed to spot the Madoff scheme before the actual collapse? Most people cannot, and that is how the scheme got to be so large (And those of you who claim you could've spotted it, where the hell where you when we needed you?). So if most financial scams

---

91   Or Fidelity, or Vanguard or Etrade, or T Rowe Price. It doesn't matter for this story.

are hard, if not impossible, to identify before it is too late, how can you protect yourself?

Enter *administrative diversification*. We have learned to diversify over time with dollar cost averaging, through different sectors of the market, through many investment types, and varying levels of risk. Perhaps it is time we looked to expand our diversification practices even further by spreading our funds among two or three different institutions.

Bernard L. Madoff Investment Securities, LLC, collapsed in 2008 unveiling an enormous Ponzi scheme, leaving a wake of fraud valued somewhere between $10 billion and $65 *billion*.[92] While this example is the extreme, there are smaller instances of investors left high and dry. Take Reserve Management's "Primary Fund" – the now notorious money market fund that "broke the buck" in September 2008 when its assets fell to 97 cents for every dollar an investor put in.[93] Frustrated investors looking for the supposedly accessible cash were told their funds were frozen.

The same thing happened to investors in the Principal U.S. Property Separate Account, which held several commercial real estate properties that proved rather hard to sell when the market took a down turn. The fund simply told investors they couldn't get their money. In a way, this creates a double loss. Not only do you take a market hit, but you also take an administrative hit by not having access to your *own* money. I'm sure many of these investors wished they had practiced a wee bit of administrative diversification to cover those short term expenses.

Even some funds that were not at risk began imposing frustrating administrative changes. In March 2009, State Street limited participants to withdrawing only 2%-4% of their money per month. State Street's argument was that in order to protect all fund investors, they needed to slow down the mad dash for the exits that often comes with a plunging market. While this is a legitimate argument, investors who assumed one level of access to their cash were rather upset when they realized they had another.

---

92 Depending on who you ask, the lawyers for the plaintiffs or the Securities and Exchange Commission.
93 A money market fund is a mutual fund that only invests in the money market, which as you now know, is a market for short-term debt. Shares in a money market fund are <u>always</u> supposed to be priced at $1. The fund pays you interest on the shares you own. For shares to drop below $1 a share is a *big* deal.

The downside to administrative diversification (aside from losing the obvious convenience of one stop shopping) is that you may lose out on some of the "bulk discounts" the financial world offers for grouping your money with one shop. Most banks will start waving fees once your balance exceeds a certain level and most insurance companies will offer a discount if your home and auto are both housed with them.

It is then the classic debate of risk verses reward. The Madoff scheme, the Primary Fund, and even the new policies at State Street showed us the risk inherent in putting all your eggs in one administrative basket. However, the savings that naturally result in bunching accounts makes it tempting.

You can always do something

At a minimum, consider moving at least some of your emergency cash fund to an institution that does not hold your other assets. While it is possible, but unlikely, that you will fall victim to the next Bernard Madoff, spreading your wealth around just a little bit could hardly do you wrong.

Chapter 36

HOW TO PROTECT AGAINST DOOMSDAY

There's been a lot of talk about doomsday and not just from the Mayans. Many folks argue we are on the verge of a financial doomsday. Those prophets can pretty much be divided into two camps:[94]

1. Those who believe we are headed for massive *deflation*

2. Those who believe we are headed for massive *inflation*

The Deflation Argument

Deflation happens when prices go down. Normally we look forward to hot dogs, sweater vests, and cell phones costing less. But with deflation, *everything* goes down: wages, home values, and stocks. As wages drop, people buy less, even though prices are down. When people buy less, companies produce less. When a business produces less, it doesn't need as many workers, so it lays people off. More layoffs mean people are spending even *less* money. And round and round we go.

The arguments for deflation are the following:

- **Baby Boomers will be retiring.** The largest, richest generation in history will be moving over to fixed incomes when they retire. They will watch their pennies. They will try to pay down their debts, rather than increasing them, as they have done for the last 30 years. Less spending will mean lower demand, fewer jobs, therefore less spending. Repeat.

---

94 And when we combine these two together, we get *stagflation,* which occurs when an economy has, high inflation, high unemployment and low growth. Don't worry. The investments discussed in this Chapter will protect against that too.

- **All consumers will be paying down debts.** On the surface, this sounds like a good thing. After all, isn't that what people like me have been yapping about for years? While debt pay down is good, it actually *isn't* good for the short-term economy because it means a pullback on spending. Less spending will mean lower demand, fewer – eh, you've heard this before.

- **Corporations will be paying down and writing off debts.** As corporations pay down the debts they owe, the less money that gets into the economy. But banks can also write off the debts owed to them. If a bank lent you $200,000 to buy a home and you can't make your payments, they will take back your home through foreclosure. If they can only sell it for $150,000, they will write off the $50,000 difference as a loss. That write-off means that money is out of our economic system forever. Which means less money goes to the shareholders. Which means the shareholders have less to spend. Less spending means – okay, I'll shut up.

- **The Federal Reserve won't go that far.** Deflation sages believe that the Fed will never print the amount of money needed to head off deflation. To do so would ruin the currency, making the US Dollar almost worthless.

The Inflation Argument

Inflation is the opposite of deflation. Prices rise. Wages will rise, too, but historically not as fast as prices. As stuff gets more expensive, consumers tend to buy less because their wages aren't rising as quickly. To help, the government prints more money and pushes it into the economy through stimulus programs. But as they print more dollars, the value of *every* dollar goes down, meaning the dollars lose their purchasing power. So stuff gets even *more* expensive. But wages don't go up as fast, so people buy less, so more money is pumped in, and dollars go down in value. Round and round we go.

The arguments for inflation are:

- **Governments are pouring a record number of stimulus dollars into the economy:** The Housing and Economic Recovery Act of 2008, TARP (Troubled Asset Relief Program) all cost bajillions that we don't technically have, so we print it.

- **Politically, printing money is more fun:** No one wants to raise taxes. No one wants to cut benefits. So option three, print more money, is what politicians usually choose. It does create inflation, but that is much more difficult for voters to spot than higher taxes or fewer benefits.

- **We've made too many promises:** Social Security, Medicare, Medicaid, and a host of other government programs can't easily be shut off or even scaled back. We have to pay for them somehow.

- **Yes, the Federal Reserve *will* go that far:** Inflation wizards believe the Fed will print all the money they need to divert this crisis, even if it ruins the currency (as did the governments of Zimbabwe, Weimar Germany, and Brazil, to name a few).

So who is right?

Well before we get there, here's where both camps agree:

- **They both don't like the Federal Reserve:** This may not help your wallet right away, but they do agree here.

- **They both think real estate will have more renters:** Either the credit markets will tighten so much that no one will be able to get a loan (argument from the deflation camp) or interest rates will be so high no one will be able to get a loan (the inflation camp.)

- **They both think the stock market will go *down*.** Both camps agree people will buy less stuff, which means corporate profits will be lower. People also will sell stocks to pay for everyday expenses.

- **Taxes will go up:** We need more revenue, and as politically unattractive as this is, it has to happen sooner or later.

- **Income, either from a job or business, will be important:** Both camps see unemployment going up, so those with a job will do well.

So what do I do, Pete?

I wish I was smart enough to tell you who is right, but I'm not.[95] I've read the books from both camps, books written by very smart people, who make very convincing arguments, with seemingly precise historical data. The good news is that you can do it all. Start with what they agree on:

- **Be as aggressive as you can paying off adjustable rate debt.**
- **Hire a tax professional to focus on *strategy*, not just preparation.**
- **Get a job or stand out in your current one.[96]**
- **If you can get it at a *super* deal, a rental property will work well. Even if the price goes down, the amount of renters should go up regardless of who is right.**

Then consider these investments:

- Purchase silver coins using the "future gift" strategy outlined in Chapter 29. If the inflation guys are right, it will rise. If they deflation guys are right, you have purchased all the gifts you need for family and friends.

- Be sure that your portfolio is balanced, that an amount equal to your age is in the safe stuff.

- If you are worried about stocks, moving some of your money to bigger established dividend paying companies – Walmart's, Pepsico's, and Kraft's of the world – or funds that buy these companies, is a good bet for both inflation and deflation, because people don't cut back on this stuff. The inflation camp also likes foreign stocks.

- Want more recommendations? Just turn the page.

---

95 At least I admit that.
96 Of course, easier said than done, but hopefully the techniques in Chapter 27 will help.

You can always do something

"Crash," "Doom" and "Depression" are words I typically associate with my dating life. But with the recent craziness in the economy, it's only natural to be worried and skeptical. When you look deeper and see that very smart people have very convincing but completely opposite arguments, it's easy to shout "Why bother?" But read through the books and you can find the similarities that will help regardless. And remember, the losers can only go to zero. There is no limit on the winners.

Chapter 37

PUTTING IT ALL TOGETHER

Are we done yet?

Almost. We've covered a lot of information from all corners of the financial world. Unfortunately, this is the only way to do it, because it can be costly to skip over something. So if your head is spinning, let me try to summarize it all into one simple chapter. You can even take these steps week by week.

Week one:

- Fill out those goal sheets.
- Fill out those net worth worksheets and the resources worksheet.
- Lighten up.

Week two:

- Start the three list exercise in Chapter 4.
- Visit unclaimed.org to see if you are entitled to any money.
- Sign up for upromise.com, babymint.com, and Igive.com.
- Get your credit report from www.annualcreditreport.com and, if necessary, get started on building it back up.
- Create an account on www.treasurydirect.gov.

Week three:

- Set up your emergency fund account. Do this either through treasurydirect.gov or some bank account that will not be easy to get money out of.
    - Arrange to have money, either from your paycheck or from your current checking account, be sent to this account. I suggest starting with 10% of your take home pay. Can't swing it? Fine, start with something smaller, but *start.*
- Visit human resources at your company. Ask them:
    - All about their retirement account (if you haven't already). If they have matching, sign up.
    - About health insurance. If your company is not offering it, reread Chapter 6 on how to get it on your own. Perhaps by getting temporary or catastrophe insurance.
    - About what other perks they have that you could be taking advantage of.
    - If you are in their retirement plan, get a copy of your most recent statement (or print this online if you can).
    - How their disability coverage works. If it does *not* cover at least 60%-80% of your income until you turn 65, you need supplemental coverage. Ask them about how to get that.
- Ask family and friends who they use to prepare their taxes. Make an appointment with this person and develop a tax strategy.

Week four:

- Call three car/homeowners insurance companies and ask for quotes. Switch if necessary.
- If you a homeowner in trouble, call the 800 number on your bank's website and start a conversation.
- Get renter's insurance if you don't have it.

- View your portfolio. Remember:
  - An amount, equal to your age, needs to be in "safe" investments. They are:
    - A cash value life insurance policy (if this works for you)
    - Government bonds you intend to hold until maturity
    - Cash accounts (money markets, bank accounts, etc.)
    - Debt you pay down more aggressively
  - The rest needs to be in "growth" investments. They are:
    - U.S. stocks/stock funds
    - Foreign stocks/stock funds
    - Real estate
    - Real estate mutual funds
    - Gold and silver (using the "future gift strategy" from Chapter 29)
  - Rearrange your investments to align with your age. On both the safe and growth side, you can split stuff up evenly. So if 50% of your money should be in growth, that 100%, on the growth side, you could divide like:
    - U.S. stocks/stock funds 20%
    - Foreign stocks/stock funds 20%
    - Real estate (paying down a rental property) 20%
    - Real estate mutual funds 20%
    - Physical gold and silver; gold and silver ETFS 20%

- If you are particularly weary of one area, say gold and silver, then you can cut back on that and put more into the other areas.

- The mix of the safe stuff isn't as important, what's important to know is how quickly you can get your money. Paying down debt is safe, but you can't get your cash back once it's done.

- When you have a minute, visit www.magicformulainvesting.com. Also read Joel Greenblatt's book, *The Little Book That Beats The Market*.

- If you are in the market for a rental property, sign up for auto email alerts from a real estate agent.

- **For the rest of your life:**
  - Review your goals once a year
  - Rebalance the portfolio based on your age or any obscene market downturns/upswings (Review three times per year)
  - Check your credit report (At least once a year)
  - Shop around your insurance (At least every two years.)
  - Commit to making one extra payment per year on all your debts (house, car, credit cards etc.)

You can always do something

I admit we covered a lot. Start with the small stuff, heck even start with the fun stuff like www.unclaimed.org and then slowly move to the other things. You'll get there.

Closing

ORDINARY THINGS, EXTRAORDINARY MOMENTS.

I began this book with a true story about my dating life, so I suppose I should end it with one as well.

Changing the names to protect the innocent, let's call her Audrey. No wait. Let's call her, Isabella. I like that better. More exotic. She was in my fifth grade class and my desk, though two rows away, still faced hers and hers mine. (I don't have time to explain the room configuration. It was weird but it worked. It worked especially well for the guys who got to look at Isabella.)

I was too chicken to approach her, and even if I hadn't been, I had no idea of what to say anyway. Fifth grade for me was when everyone was just starting to interact (in that way) with the enemy camp. Somehow a rumor leaked (or maybe I leaked) that I liked Isabella, and a happy conspiracy was formed, behind my back, for us to dance at the one (and only) dance of fifth grade.

Right from the start, I f'ed the whole thing up. She put her arms around my neck and I, uhhh ... following her lead, I put *my* arms around *her* neck. I know now my hands were supposed to be around her waist, but keep in mind that A) I was clueless and B) I was in fifth grade at my first dance and C) I was also on cloud nine.

The song, if you are curious, was *Hungry Eyes* by Eric Carmen.[97] It certainly had all the merits of a good slow dance song, save for its brevity.

---

97 *Dirty Dancing* fans will remember this song from the film.

The lighting was terrible, and by terrible I mean it was a brightly lit cafeteria. As I stated, our dancing was off, and yours truly was to blame.

But standing that close to Isabella made all that not matter. My heart roared in anticipation of that dance. It roared when I put my arms around her, or rather, her neck, and it roared for the entire weekend afterward. Had my parents known this, they could have bestowed upon me an infinite supply of chores, cleaning attics, garages and cars and all of it would have been done with a cheerful smile. Perhaps they even *did* subject me to this labor and I cannot recall a lick of it.

That whole weekend I thought of nothing but Isabella. That's when, as a fifth grader, I realized:

There are no ordinary moments.

One More

Before I get to my point, allow me one more story. This story is about the greatest meal of my life.

The greatest meal of my life did *not* occur on the Orient Express while crossing from Italy into France. It did *not* occur at the Hotel Plaza Athenee in Paris, or in the Fairmont Copley Plaza Hotel in Boston, or in at the Commander's Palace in New Orleans. It was not at the Movenpick Hotel in the Kingdom of Bahrain; it was not prepared by my *private* chef while on safari in the Serengeti, nor was it served up by the private chef I dated (not the one from the Serengeti). It was not that $250 per person restaurant I ate at in Tokyo, the name of which I still cannot recall.

Rather, the greatest meal of my life occurred at a small restaurant called The Tilton Diner, a bit of a dive, just off exit 20 on Route 93 in Tilton, New Hampshire. I was a senior in high school, and I had a hot chocolate and a tuna melt.

During the three hours before I settled down to the greatest meal of my life, I was participating in one of the most exhausting experiences of my life. My friends and I had written a play that we were producing, directing, and acting in as our senior project. (Our school allowed, and even encouraged, senior projects.) For those of you unfamiliar with the term, "Senior Project" is a condensed academic term for "legally-blowing-off-the-last 6-weeks-of-your-senior-year-of-high-school." Students can opt to dive deeper into a particular subject area provided their senior year grades were up to par. Somehow, mine were.[98]

The script of the play called for a crashed plane as one of the sets. Our faculty advisor was certainly hoping for a "pretend" plane. But my incurably stubborn friend spent an entire morning on the phone until he found an airplane junkyard with an old Cessna that we could borrow for the show.

The airplane junkyard was just off Route 93 in Tilton, New Hampshire.

My dad had a trailer that could hook up to his station wagon, and offering very little information, I persuaded him to let me borrow it. Shortly after hitching it up, I picked up my friend, and we eased into the 50-minute drive to the airplane junkyard.

I can't remember the guy's name, but I think it was Skip. He showed us the plane he referenced on the phone. It lay rather far away from his office and, if memory serves, he informed us he was running out for a few hours, but we were free to take the plane.

That's when it started to rain.

A Cessna without an engine is light, and the two of us got it easy enough onto the trailer. The trouble was that the trailer door wouldn't shut, and we realized we would have to disassemble the plane into two parts.

That's when we realized we didn't have a tool box.

Trying to unbolt a rusted bolt with your bare hands is next to impossible. We took turns. One man would try to loosen the bolt with his water logged fingers while the other man mined the airplane graveyard for something that could be used as a wrench.

The answer was two pieces of metal that could be pinched together to form a crude vice grip, that, in turn, could (somehow) loosen a bolt. It took *three hours* in the pouring rain to loosen *five* bolts. Our hands were numb, sliced to shreds on the edges of the razor sharp aircraft aluminum, and our clothes were soaked. We were starving, freezing and angry.

---

98 Most likely due to a glitch in the school's computer system.

Exhausted once the final bolt came undone, we heaved the two halves of the plane onto the trailer, shut the back gate and drove in search of the nearest restaurant. We stumbled, waterlogged into the Tilton Diner, and I had the greatest meal of my life.

There are no ordinary moments.

Now let me tell you what I *cannot* remember

I cannot remember the first nice watch I owned, or the second. When I got my first laptop computer, I believe it was a Dell, but I cannot tell you the hard drive space, the monitor size, the RAM, or the speed. As a child growing up, I had some Polo shirts, some Lacoste shirts, and some shirts that were hand me downs from my brother. I have no clue which ones, if any, were important to me. I believe my first cell phone was a Samsung, but I cannot be sure of that. As I write this, I am wearing my favorite pair of shoes, but I can't tell you which brand they are without looking. They're just comfortable.

There are ordinary things.

Try this exercise yourself. Think of your fondest memories. The ones that truly made you smile. Most likely it was an experience or a moment rather than a thing. Even if it was a thing, like a car, chances are it wasn't the car itself but the experiences that car brought you - the freedom, the independence, or the fact that you don't have to sit next to that creepy guy on the bus.

I am not making this stuff up. There's a dude who actually researched this, and I actually met the dude. His name is Dr. Ryan Howell. He argues that we gain more pleasure by spending money on experiences – travel, dinners with friends – than we do spending our money on jewelry, clothes and electronics. Google him and remember:

There are no ordinary moments, but there are ordinary things.

We often kill ourselves to get flashier cars, bigger houses, and better clothes under the belief that these things will make us happier. But they won't. What will make us happier is recognizing the magic that occurs in the world every day and taking a moment to appreciate it. Cheesy, but true.

I could go on and on with the magical moments I remember. Like I could tell you the story of the *greatest* pickup line of my life, which occurred in a clothing store in Jackson Hole, Wyoming, many years ago. Interestingly enough, it was in the *same* year I crashed and burned with the worst pickup line of my life. The pickup was done using a three-man formation known as the "Dual Rotating Wingman." Nearly impossible to pull off, but very effective when successful, it certainly worked much better than my tango with Charlotte.

But that, dear reader, is another story.

WHO IS THIS GUY?

Peter Bielagus is a former financial advisor who now travels the world speaking to students, professionals and service members about changing their financial lives. He has spoken in Italy, Greece, Spain, Japan, Korea, the Middle East, as well as every state except North Dakota and Alaska. If you are located in North Dakota or Alaska, please hire him to speak, as he is tired of clarifying that those are the only two states he has not spoken in. He has even spoken on an aircraft carrier while at sea, somewhere in the Indian Ocean.

Peter is the author of two (now three!) books on money management. His first book *Getting Loaded: Make a Million While You're Still Young Enough to Enjoy It*, was published by Penguin Putnam/NAL. His second book, *Quick Cash for Teens: Be Your Own Boss and Make Big Bucks*, an entrepreneurship guide for teenagers, was published by Sterling Publishing.

Known for mixing humor and emotion with real life examples, Peter serves up simple, practical, and profound financial strategies in his books and talks. A frequent guest of the media, he has been featured in the Wall Street Journal, USA Today, The Miami Herald, and was a guest on the PBS show *Your Life, Your Money*.

He lives in New Hampshire and is currently dating his carry-on suitcase, whom he has taken all over the world.

JOIN MY EMAIL NEWSLETTER:

If you liked the tips, tricks and jokes contained in this book, you can keep them coming by signing up for my newsletter. Delivered once a week either in text or video format, you can read it/watch it in less than two minutes.

Sign up at www.peterbielagus.com.

BTW you can email me through this website as well. If you have a financial question that for any reason was not answered in this book, please email me and I will try my best to get back to you as soon as I can.

You can also find me on facebook @gettingloaded and on twitter @gettingloaded.

I look forward to staying in touch!

INTERESTED IN HAVING PETER
SPEAK TO YOUR ORGANIZATION?

For the past seven years, Peter has traveled the globe, educating and entertaining audiences to take charge of their financial lives. His past clients include: all branches of the United States Military, Wealthmasters International, The Main Society of CPAs, The Access Group, The New Hampshire Higher Education Funding Association, Harvard Law School and over 100 colleges and universities throughout the country. He is known for making finance fun, and showing people of all incomes just how much they really have.

For bulk book orders and speaking availability, please call our office at 866-673-3152 or visit us on our website at www.peterbielagus.com.

CPSIA information can be obtained at www.ICGtesting.com
Printed in the USA
BVOW05s2045231114

376093BV00002B/5/P

9 781467 515801